Civil Society

Third Edition

For Cora
My own "civil society"

CIVIL SOCIETY

Third Edition

Michael Edwards

polity

First edition published in 2004 by Polity Press
Second edition published in 2009 by Polity Press
This third edition first published in 2014 by Polity Press
Reprinted 2014, 2015(twice), 2016, 2017(twice)

Polity Press
65 Bridge Street
Cambridge CB2 1UR, UK

Polity Press
350 Main Street
Malden, MA 02148, USA

ISBN-13: 978-0-7456-7935-8
ISBN-13: 978-0-7456-7936-5 (pb)

A catalogue record for this book is available from the British Library.

Typeset in 11 on 13 pt Berling
by Toppan Best-set Premedia Limited
Printed and bound in USA by LSC Communications

The publisher has used its best endeavours to ensure that the URLs for external websites referred to in this book are correct and active at the time of going to press. However, the publisher has no responsibility for the websites and can make no guarantee that a site will remain live or that the content is or will remain appropriate.

Every effort has been made to trace all copyright holders, but if any have been inadvertently overlooked the publisher will be pleased to include any necessary credits in any subsequent reprint or edition.

For further information on Polity, visit our website: www.polity.co.uk

Contents

Preface

Since the first edition of this book was published in 2004, the number of searches for "civil society" recorded by Google each year has fallen by 70 percent[1] – not a particularly rigorous indicator of interest and support perhaps, but surprising to those like me who once saw civil society as "the big idea for the century to come," as I put it in my original Preface. Of course, people still organize themselves for voluntary, collective action, and episodes like the "Arab Spring" continue to hit the headlines, only to subside into less intense activity once the streets and squares have been cleared of protestors and police. Perhaps this is inevitable given that such bursts of civic energy are difficult to sustain after their immediate causes have been addressed, and in the face of widespread repression and insecurity. As I write this Preface the same script is being re-enacted in Istanbul's Taksim Square and across the cities of Brazil – met, as usual, by tear gas and batons rather than by greater openness to reforms. Even the few positive attempts by politicians to nurture civic action have receded, with Britain's "Big Society" getting smaller by the day, and little sign that widespread grassroots participation in Barack Obama's re-election campaign has had any impact on the willingness of his government to pursue a more radical agenda in the USA.

To me, however, these facts change little about the significance of civil society in the long-term evolution of politics and culture. The reality of activism in most settings has always been less glamorous than the headlines may suggest, and strong social movements are comparatively rare. The power that people have to shape their societies is usually channeled through their day-to-day participation in voluntary associations and communities; churches, mosques and synagogues; labor unions, political parties and other expressions of "normal" civic life. In chapter 2, I use the metaphor of civil society as an iceberg with its peaks above the waterline in the form of high-profile organizations and events, and the great mass of civic interaction hidden underneath. Examples like the Arab Spring are significant in and of themselves, but perhaps of longer-term importance is what is happening below the surface. Since the early 2000s there is increasing evidence that much of the "ice" is melting as face-to-face civic interaction becomes less popular or more difficult to sustain. Or perhaps the "iceberg" is simply reshaping itself under the influence of new developments in technology, social media and the market, with consequences for civil society that may be positive, negative, or somewhere in between. It is these longer-term, subterranean developments that are the focus of the third edition of this book.

One of the benefits of revising a manuscript at regular intervals is that new ideas and interpretations can be added along the way. I have received a good deal of critical feedback from readers who have used this book in academic courses, commissions of inquiry, policy-making processes, public education, and strategic planning for non-governmental organizations (NGOs), foundations and other donor agencies. So in this revision I have added two new sections on subjects that have developed rapidly since the second edition was produced in 2009. The first concerns the overlaps between civil society and the market that are producing an interesting breed of hybrid institution variously known as social enterprises or social entrepreneurs, backed up by "venture philanthropy," "impact investing" and other forms of financing that are heavily influenced by business thinking. These issues are treated in chapter 3 as a potentially important shift in the ways in which we understand the constitution of the good society.

The second set of developments revolve around social media and the increasing use of information and communication technologies (ICTs) in civic interaction – probably the most talked-about phenomenon in the civil society debate in recent years. Such technologies, and the shifts in communication they facilitate, have the potential to greatly expand at least some parts of the public sphere, and so they are dealt with in chapter 4. Both these trends have implications for civil society that are thoroughly ambiguous, and healthily contested. In addition, new material has been added to the geographical essays in chapter 2, and I have tried to answer some well-targeted criticisms that my original treatment of civil society in the Middle East and Africa was too reliant on a limited understanding of ascriptive versus cross-cutting associations and relationships. New social movements or bursts of movement activity among both progressive and conservative forces are also covered in chapter 2, while chapter 4 explores in more detail emerging forms of participatory democracy, in which civil society has a central role to play. Finally, I have updated the case studies, data, examples and references used throughout.

As this book has evolved since the early 2000s I have come to appreciate two longer-term trends that underpin all the different revisions, and that now run more clearly throughout the text. The first is the absolute necessity of building, sustaining and revitalizing the infrastructure of citizen action at the grassroots level, without which civil society cannot function in any of its guises. If it is worth telling, the story of civil society has to be written not by bureaucrats or billionaires, but by millions of ordinary people who wish to rearrange the "geometry of human relationships" in ways that speak to their visions of the good society.[2] The creation of civil society is a human drama, not a technical exercise in government planning or a supply chain in a business in which inputs and outputs can be manipulated and controlled. Otherwise there is little hope that citizens will be able to hold power to account from a position of independence, or come together to determine their own futures other than as recipients of top-down direction and the incentives of the market.

It is particularly important those most affected by poverty and discrimination are able to express themselves directly in civil society action so that voluntary associations, political participation, and public debates are not dominated by groups claiming to act on their behalf. And that means protecting and enhancing the self-governing organizations that have always formed the core of civic interaction, through which the mass of the population can activate their energies as creative citizens. The homogenizing of civil society ecosystems discussed in chapters 2, 3 and 5 – variously described in terms of corporatization, NGO-ization and greater bureaucracy – poses a special threat to the collective action capacities of low-income and other marginalized communities, as exemplified by the attempted destruction of the labor movement in the USA, for example, or the dramatic decline in support for community organizing among philanthropic foundations. Yet it is precisely this hard, basic, civic or public work that is most under threat today from a combination of widespread economic insecurity, rising individualism and inequality in every sphere of life, political repression and increasing government surveillance, and the popularity of celebrity humanitarians, billionaire philanthropists and the hype-merchants of social media and the market, who apply a sheen that gilds the surface of civil society in many countries but who do little to build it at its core. Unglamorous, unheralded and often unsupported, this is the civil society we simply cannot afford to lose, since we cannot achieve anything that is of real value to all of us by working as individuals, however successful, but only through collective action, like an orchestra instead of a brilliant soloist or a tapestry instead of a few rich threads.

Second, every generation faces the challenge of nurturing civil society against the background of a new set of circumstances and supplied with a different set of tools. Ideally, it should be possible to take advantage of new tools like social markets and social media without disavowing what is valuable from the past – like the value of face-to-face interaction and democratic governance. But in reality this seems difficult to accomplish, perhaps because we are constantly searching for new magic bullets that can resolve the problems of declining civic participation and engagement, or because we over-estimate the benefits of anything that is new when there are reputations and fortunes to be made. During the same nine-year period in which Google searches for "civil society" fell by 70 percent, searches for "social media"[3] and "social entrepreneurs"[4] rose by 90 percent and 40 percent respectively, a clear indicator of changing fashions.

There is no doubt that these developments open up important opportunities to strengthen associational life and the health of the public sphere, or that they could help to achieve a better synthesis of online and offline organizing, bonding and bridging social ties, and self-funding and commercial revenue generation for non-profits. But as later chapters make clear, there are also many conflicts and trade-offs involved in the adoption of these new ideas which must be carefully interrogated, free from the exaggeration of their enthusiasts and the nostalgia of their critics. I suspect that face-to-face public work is always going to be more powerful than social media or market opportunities in pursuing civil society's core functions, and that new moral revolutions will continue to be organized in the flesh, whichever tools we use to communicate with each other and raise funds to do our work.

Finally, in the years to come I have no doubt that civil society will be repressed or weakened in many places, just as it will be celebrated and strengthened in many others. This is the reality of punch and counter-punch wherever power relations are contested and remade. Collective action is in our DNA as social beings, and there is never a shortage of causes and opportunities to put our collective energies into practice. Intense mobilizations will continue to flame up in response to authoritarian regimes, rising inequality and injustice, but the real task is to sustain them over time – to sustain the preconditions for people to shape civil society for themselves, as I put in it in chapter 6. Only then will a strong civil society become the norm rather than the exception. People will adjust the tools and techniques they use to do these things as circumstances change, and they may have to relearn or re-adapt some of the skills of collective action for the contexts that lie ahead. Will the patterns of civic engagement that emerge from this process be very different, and will those differences prove significant for the larger questions of democracy and freedom in "societies that are civil"? That is the question I hope this book will help you to understand and answer.

Acknowledgments

My thanks go to all those who have provided feedback on the second edition of *Civil Society* since its publication in 2009, and who have supplied me with a rich array of additional references, case studies and other source material. Naturally, responsibility for all errors and omissions in the book remains mine alone. I have received excellent support and guidance from Jonathan Skerrett and Elen Griffiths at Polity Press in Cambridge. The revisions for this book were completed at our home in upstate New York, where my wife Cora is blazing a trail for true democracy and decency in government. As my own "civil society," this book continues to be dedicated to her.

Michael Edwards
Swan Hill
June 2013

1
Introduction –
What's the Big Idea?

Set into the wall of the Church of the Ascension on London's Blackheath is a small metal plaque. "Fellowship is life," it reads, "and lack of fellowship is death, but in hell there is no brotherhood but every man for himself." John Ball, the leader of the Peasants' Revolt who spoke these words nearby in 1381, would not have thought of himself as part of "civil society," but his sentiments have been echoed down the centuries by anyone who has ever joined a group, formed an association or volunteered to defend or advance the causes they believe in. Collective action in search of the good society is a universal part of human experience, though manifested in a million different ways across time, space and culture. In Sullivan County, New York, where I live, I am surrounded by contemporary examples of the same phenomenon – the volunteer fire service, the free give-away of hay to those who can't afford to buy it for their pets, the music sale by Radio W-JEFF ("America's only hydro-powered public radio station"), the Eileen Haworth Weil Scholarship Fund celebrating local activists, and a myriad of other groups catering to every affinity and interest. Yet Sullivan County remains economically depressed and politically dysfunctional, one more set of communities on the margins of a nation that is increasingly violent, unequal and apparently incapable of resolving its own pressing social problems. A strong civil society, it seems, is no guarantee that society will be strong and civil.

Concepts of civil society have a rich history, but it is only since the early 1980s that they have moved to the center of the international stage. There are a number of reasons for this development – the fall of communism and the democratic openings that followed, disenchantment with the economic and political models of the past, a yearning for togetherness in a world that seems ever-more insecure, and the rapid rise of non-governmental organizations (NGOs) on the global stage. Today, civil society is a little less popular as a generalized "solution" to these problems, but it remains high on the agendas of government officials, journalists, funding agencies, writers and academics, not to mention the millions of people across the globe who see it as an inspiration in their struggles for a better world. Cited as a key element of social progress by politicians and thinkers from left, right and all perspectives in between, civil society is claimed by every part of the ideological spectrum as its own, but what exactly is it?

"Civil society," says the libertarian Cato Institute in Washington, DC, means "fundamentally reducing the role of politics in society by expanding free markets and individual liberty."[1] This will surprise those on the left who see it as the seedbed for radical social movements. The Advocacy Institute, one of Cato's alter egos, calls civil society "the best way forward for politics in the post-Cold War world," "a society that protects those who organize to challenge power" and "the single most viable alternative to the authoritarian state and the tyrannical market."[2] Not to be outdone, those in the middle ground of politics claim that civil society – by gently correcting generations of state and market failure – could be the missing link in the success of social democracy. Meanwhile, back in academia, civil society has become the "chicken soup of the social sciences" – "the new analytic key that will unlock the mysteries of the social order." The American writer Jeremy Rifkin calls civil society "our last, best hope";

UK politicians of every stripe see it as central to holding society together against the onrush of globalizing markets; the United Nations and the World Bank see it as one of the keys to "good governance" and poverty-reducing growth; and – lest one sees this as a giant Western conspiracy – here is the autumn 2002 edition of China's semi-official news magazine *Huasheng Shidian* plagiarizing the American scholar Lester Salamon: "the role of NGOs in the twenty-first century will be as significant as the role of the nation-state in the twentieth." These are strange bedfellows with ambitious dreams, but can they all be right?

Such chameleon-like qualities are not unique to "civil society," but when the same phrase is used to justify such radically different viewpoints it is certainly time to ask some deeper questions about what is going on. After all, an idea that means everything probably signifies nothing. At the very least, clarity about the different understandings in play is necessary if we are to a have a sensible conversation, yet a glance through the civil society literature would leave most people thoroughly confused. Depending on whose version one follows, civil society is either a specific product of the nation-state and capitalism that arose spontaneously to mediate conflicts between social life and the market economy when the industrial revolution fractured traditional bonds of kin and community; or a universal expression of the collective life of individuals that is at work in all countries and stages of development, but one that is expressed in different ways according to history and culture. Since nation-states in much of the developing world are largely a colonial creation, civil societies in the South are bound to differ from those that emerged in the North.

Some see civil society as one of three sectors (along with the state and the market), separate from and independent of each other though sometimes overlapping in the middle. Others emphasize the "fuzzy" borders and interrelationships that exist between these sectors, increasingly characterized by hybrids of various kinds. Some claim that only certain associations are part of civil society – voluntary, democratic, modern and civil according to some pre-defined set of normative criteria – while others insist that all associations qualify for membership, including "uncivil" society and traditional associations that are based on inherited characteristics such as ethnicity. Are families "in" or "out" of civil society, and what about the business sector? Is civil society a bulwark against the state, an indispensable support for government reformers, or dependent on state intervention for its existence? Is it the key to individual freedom through the guaranteed experience of pluralism or a threat to democracy through special-interest politics? Is it a noun (a part of society), an adjective (a kind of society), an arena for societal deliberation or a mixture of all three?

It is not difficult to find support for any of these positions, and we will hear much more about the different arguments later in the book. But what is to be done with a concept that seems so unsure of itself that definitions are akin to nailing jelly to the wall? One response would be to ditch the concept completely, but this would be a mistake. Although the civil society debate is "riddled with ethnocentric assumptions developed in conditions that don't exist anywhere in the contemporary world," is "no longer based on any coherent theory or principles," has been reduced to "an ideological rendezvous for erstwhile antagonists," and is therefore "ineffective as a model for social and political practice," both the theory and practice of citizen action are alive and kicking in the worlds of politics, public policy, activism and foreign aid.[3] Therefore, "the resultant intellectual confusion could well wreak havoc on the real world given the fact that civil societies have now been recognized as a legitimate area for external intervention."[4] Conceptual clarity, analytical rigor, empirical authenticity, policy relevance and emancipatory potential are all threatened when civil society becomes a slogan. But selective scorn, scholarly admonishment and attempts to enforce a universal consensus are unlikely to resolve this problem.

What, therefore, is the best way forward? I think it lies through greater clarity and rigor, so that different interpretations of civil society can be debated on their merits. Without clarity and rigor, theories of civil society will be a poor guide to public policy and citizen action, whatever the values and goals at stake. At the very least, rigor can expose dogma that masquerades as truth, and challenge policy-makers who have an ideological axe to grind. And, as I try to show in the chapters that follow, ideas about civil society can prosper in a rigorous critique so long as we are prepared to abandon false universals, magic bullets and painless panaceas. The goal of this book is not consensus (something that would be impossible to achieve in the civil society debate) but greater clarity. And greater clarity, I hope, can be the basis for a better conversation in the future.

Civil society: a very brief history of an idea

The first step in achieving greater clarity is to identify the origins of different contemporary understandings of civil society in the history of political thought. This is not a theoretical book, or a book about civil society theory; but to appreciate the ways in which theory has been muddled and misapplied in practice a quick tour through theory is essential. As Keynes's famous dictum reminds us, "practical men in authority who think themselves immune from theoretical influences are usually the slaves of some defunct economist," just as present-day "civil-society builders" are motivated, consciously or not, by ideas that are deeply rooted in the past.

Fortunately, we are blessed with a number of books that provide excellent and detailed accounts of the history of this idea.[5] They show how civil society has been a point of reference for philosophers since antiquity in their struggle to understand the great issues of the day: the nature of the good society, the rights and responsibilities of citizens, the practice of politics and government, and, most especially, how to live together peacefully by reconciling our individual autonomy with our collective aspirations, balancing freedom and its boundaries, and marrying pluralism with conformity so that complex societies can function with both efficiency and justice. Such questions were difficult enough to resolve in small, homogeneous communities where face-to-face social interaction could build reciprocity and trust, but in an increasingly integrated world where none of these conditions apply they become hugely more demanding. Yet the discussions that took place in the ferment of the Arab Spring during 2011 and 2012 would surely have been familiar to Aristotle, Hobbes, Ferguson, de Tocqueville, Gramsci and others in the long roster of civil society thinkers that stretches back two thousand years. Though the profile of these ideas has certainly waxed and waned, arguing about civil society has always been a part of political and philosophical debate.

In classical thought, civil society and the state were seen as indistinguishable, with both referring to a type of political association that governed social conflict through the imposition of rules that restrained citizens from harming one another. Aristotle's *polis* was an "association of associations" that enabled citizens (or those few individuals that qualified) to share in the virtuous tasks of ruling and being ruled. In this sense, the state represented the "civil" form of society and "civility" described the requirements of good citizenship. Late medieval thought continued this tradition by equating civil society with the value of "politically organized commonwealths," a type of civilization made possible because people lived in law-governed associations protected by the state.[6] The alternative is social Darwinism – the "survival of the fittest."

Between 1750 and 1850, ideas about civil society took a new and fundamental turn in response to a perceived crisis in the ruling social order. This crisis was motivated by the rise of the market economy and the increasing differentiation of interests it provoked, as "communities of strangers" replaced "communities of neighbors," and by the breakdown of traditional paradigms of authority as a consequence of the French and American revolutions. In contrast to Aristotle, Plato and

Hobbes, the thinkers of the Enlightenment viewed civil society as a defense against unwarranted intrusions *by* the state on newly realized individual rights and freedoms, organized through the medium of voluntary associations. In this school of thought, civil society was a self-regulating universe of associations committed to the same ideals that needed, at all costs, to be protected from the state in order to preserve its role in resisting despotism. This was a theme taken up by a host of thinkers, including James Madison (in his *Federalist Papers*) and Alexis de Tocqueville (probably the most famous civil society enthusiast of them all), and – much later in time – by the "small circles of freedom" that were formed by dissidents in Eastern Europe, by the writers who celebrated them in the West (such as Ernest Gellner), and by academics such as Robert Putnam who began to investigate the condition of associational life and its effects in Italy, the USA and elsewhere, spawning a whole new debate on "social capital" in the process. The dominant theme in this debate was the value of voluntary associations in curbing the power of centralizing institutions, protecting pluralism and nurturing constructive social norms, especially "generalized trust and cooperation." A highly articulated civil society with overlapping memberships was seen as the foundation of a stable democratic polity, a defense against domination by any particular group, and a barrier to anti-democratic forces.[7]

Today, this "neo-Tocquevillian" tradition is particularly strong in the USA, where it dovetails naturally with pre-existing traditions of self-governance, suspicions about the state, and concerns about public disengagement from politics and civic life, and is closely linked to other schools of thought such as communitarianism, localism and the "liberal egalitarianism" of Michael Walzer, William Galston and others.[8] In contrast to classical liberals, liberal egalitarians recognize the debilitating effects of unequal access to resources and opportunities on the health and functioning of civil society. This is an important insight, and scholars have built on these ideas to construct a comprehensive critique of the neo-Tocquevillian tradition that focuses on the structural obstacles that prevent some groups from articulating their interests; the ethnocentrism or simple unreliability of assumptions about associations and their effects; and a failure to account for the impact of globalization, economic restructuring, political corruption and power relations of different kinds.[9] Even this critique, however, reaches back through history to connect with much earlier debates about the ideas that developed during the Enlightenment. Hegel was the first of these early critics, focusing on the conflicts and inequalities that raged between different economic and political interests within civil society that required constant surveillance by the state in order for the "civil" to remain. This was a theme taken further by Karl Marx, who saw civil society as another vehicle for furthering the interests of the dominant class under capitalism, and then by Antonio Gramsci – the person who "may be single-handedly responsible for the revival of the term civil society in the post-World War Two period."[10] Although Gramsci reasoned in Marxist categories, he reached some conclusions that differed from his intellectual master, since, in Gramsci's view, civil society was the site of rebellion against the orthodox as well as the construction of cultural and ideological hegemony, expressed through families, schools, universities and the media as well as voluntary associations, since all these institutions are important in shaping the political dispositions of citizens.

Philosophers in the United States such as John Dewey and Hannah Arendt took Gramsci's ideas about civil society as an arena for contestation and developed around them a theory of the "public sphere" as an essential component of democracy. By the "public," Dewey meant the shared experience of social and political life that underpinned public deliberation on the great questions of the day. Anything that eroded this public sphere – for example, the commercialization of the media or the commodification of education – was to be resisted. Such ideas continue to resonate today among Americans committed to deliberative and dialogic democracy, but it was in Europe that the theory of the public sphere reached its highest levels of articulation through the work of

Jürgen Habermas. Habermas combined the Marxist tradition that exposes domination in civil society with the liberal tradition that emphasizes its role in guarding personal autonomy, and drew these different threads together through a series of theoretical constructs concerning "communicative action," "discursive democracy" and the "colonization of the life world." For Habermas and other "critical theorists," a healthy civil society is one "that is steered by its members through shared meanings" that are constructed democratically through the communications structures of the public sphere.[11] Today, these ideas are echoed by theorists and activists on the left who see civil society as the site of progressive politics – "the social basis of a democratic public sphere through which a culture of inequality can be dismantled" – and by political philosophers such as John Keane and Jeffrey Alexander, who are attempting to construct a new vision of civil society that respects and sorts through differences between groups by simultaneously promoting non-violent engagement "from above" through state authority embedded in national constitutions and international law; and "from below" by channeling violent tendencies into non-violent associational life and through the public sphere.[12]

This whistle-stop tour through history shows that ideas about civil society have passed through many phases without ever securing a consensus, even leaving aside all the other variants of civil society thinking that I have omitted in order to focus on the basics – such as non-Western theories or theories about non-Western societies, scholarship about African-American civil society in the USA, feminist contributions to the debate, and others. I will get to these contributions a little later, though most of my analysis will be skewed toward North America and Western Europe, and the literatures they have spawned. Although work on civil society outside these contexts is growing, it has not yet reached a level at which systematic comparisons can be made. Nevertheless, there is little doubt that the civil society debate will continue to divide scholars in fundamental ways, and although such divisions are never watertight, I want to focus in the rest of the book on three contrasting schools of thought that emerge from this brief discussion of the history of ideas: civil society as a *part* of society (the neo-Tocquevillian school that focuses on associational life), civil society as a *kind* of society (characterized by positive norms and values as well as success in meeting particular social goals), and civil society as the *public sphere*. After each of these schools is explored in detail, the latter part of the book shows how they can be related to each other and where such an integrated approach might take us in terms of public policy.

Each school of thought has a respectable intellectual history and is visible in the discourse of scholars, politicians, foundations and international agencies, but it is the first – civil society as associational life – that dominates the debate. It is Alexis de Tocqueville's ghost that wanders through the corridors of the World Bank, not that of Habermas or Hegel. Indeed, the first two schools of thought are regularly conflated – it being assumed that a healthy associational life contributes to, or even produces, the "good society" in ways that are predictable – while the public sphere is usually ignored. This messy mélange of means and ends will be challenged extensively in the pages that follow, but before embarking on this investigation it is important to understand why such lazy thinking is so common. Why has this particular interpretation of civil society become so popular since the Cold War ended?

The rise and rise of civil society

There is no doubt that neo-Tocquevillian ideas about civil society have been a prime beneficiary of wider political and ideological changes that have redefined the powers and responsibilities of states, markets and voluntary associations since the early 1960s. At the broadest level, there are three ways in which societies can resolve collective problems – through rules or laws enforced by the coercive power of the state, through the unintended consequences of individual decisions in the marketplace, and through social mechanisms embedded in voluntary action, discussion and agreement. The weight attached to each of these models has shifted significantly, with state-based solutions in the ascendancy from 1945 to the mid-1970s (the era of the welfare state in the North and centralized planning in the South), and market-based solutions in pole position from the late 1970s to 1990 or thereabouts (the era of Reaganomics in the North and "structural adjustment" in the South). Disaffection with the results of both these models – the deadening effect of too much state intervention and the human consequences of an over-reliance on the market – required a new approach that addressed the consequences of both state and market failure. This new approach, which gained strength throughout the 1990s and 2000s, went by many names (including the "third way" and "compassionate conservatism"), but its central tenet is that partnership between all three sectors of society working together – public, private and civic – is the best way to overcome social and economic problems. Civil society as associational life became central to the workings of this project, and this project – as a new way of achieving social progress – became identified with building "societies that are civil."

In addition, the political changes that culminated in the fall of the Berlin Wall in 1989 gave the idea of civil society a prominence it had not enjoyed since the Enlightenment, but in a manner that also encouraged the conflation of ends with means. Civil society became both a rallying cry for dissidents – a new type of society characterized by liberal-democratic norms – and a vehicle for achieving it by building social movements strong enough to overthrow authoritarian states. The paradigm case for the conflation of these two perspectives was Solidarity in Poland (see chapter 2), though here, as elsewhere in Eastern Europe and now across the Middle East, associational life tended to be disregarded fairly quickly once the dissidents were elected into office. Nevertheless, the rise of direct democracy that was such a feature of political change in Eastern Europe, the former Soviet

Union and large parts of the developing world during the 1990s remains a trend of global importance, perhaps as important as the invention of representative democracy in the eighteenth and nineteenth centuries. As the balance between direct and representative democracy continues to shift in favor of the former – driven by disaffection with conventional politics as well as the attractions of alternative means of participation – the political role of voluntary associations as the prime vehicles for organizing such participation will continue to grow. As we shall see in later chapters, these changes bring problems as well as opportunities, but it seems unlikely that they will be reversed.

Worldwide moves toward state retrenchment and privatization have promoted new levels of personal insecurity among the majority of the world's population against a background of global market integration, increased mobility and rapid social and technological change. Modernity, as Robert Bellah reminds us, is a "culture of separation," and capitalism provides no collective identity to bring us together other than as consumers.[13] Traditional social institutions and ways of dealing with such insecurities such as welfare states, labor unions and nuclear families have been progressively dismantled during this process, leaving behind heightened levels of vulnerability and uncertainty. In these circumstances, a retreat to the familiar is to be expected, and this is exactly what voluntary associations can provide – a reassuring oasis of solidarity and mutual support among like-minded people who provide each other with emotional as well as material support, from soup kitchens to self-help to spiritual salvation. Indeed, an additional reason for the rapid rise in interest in civil society since the early 1990s has been the collection of a mounting body of evidence that suggests that associational life plays a much more important social, economic and political role than was realized in the 1970s and 1980s. Civil society has been noticed, not just because of the rising public and political profile of NGOs and other groups, but because a body of evidence now exists to justify this profile, backed by specialist expertise in universities and think-tanks and supported with large amounts of money from research funding bodies, foundations and governments.

At the level of national development performance, this evidence shows that the synergy between a strong state and a strong society is one of the keys to sustained, poverty-reducing growth, because networks of intermediary associations act as counterweights to vested interests, promote accountability in states and markets, build new and more inclusive institutions, channel information to decision-makers on what is happening at the "sharp end," and negotiate the social contracts between government and citizens that development requires – "I'll scratch your back by delivering growth, investment and services; you scratch mine by delivering wage restraint or absorbing the costs of welfare." Taiwan, one of the most successful of late industrializers, had over 8 million members in such intermediary groups by the early 1980s, including trade unions, student associations and local councils.[14]

At a more detailed level, it is useful to break down the developmental roles of civil society into three interrelated areas: economic, political and social. The economic role of civil society centers on securing livelihoods and providing services where states and markets are weak, and nurturing the social values, networks and institutions that underpin successful market economies, including trust and cooperation. As Lester Salamon has shown, voluntary associations the world over have become key providers of human services (especially health and welfare), and now constitute a 2.2 *trillion* dollar industry in just forty countries that were sampled.[15] NGOs, religious organizations and other civic groups have always been significant service providers; the difference now is that they are seen as the preferred channel for service provision in deliberate substitution for the state. In more radical formulations (such as the World Social Forum), civil society is seen as a vehicle for "humanizing capitalism" by promoting accountability among corporations, progressive social policies among governments, and new experiments in "social economics" that combine market efficiency with cooperative values.

In their social role, civil societies are seen as a reservoir of caring, cultural life and intellectual innovation, teaching people – at least according to the neo-Tocquevillians – the skills of citizenship and nurturing a collection of positive social norms that foster stability, loosely collected under the rubric of "social capital." In turn, social capital is seen as the crucial ingredient in promoting collective action for the common good, or simply creating and maintaining the social ties that are essential if individuals are to function effectively in modern economies, where the demands of exchange are growing more and more complex. The normative effects of voluntary associations lie at the core of the neo-Tocquevillian argument, though this is as much a moral as a social issue for them. In some ways this is to be expected, since many neo-Tocquevillians are conservatives, and conservatives tend to look back in time to re-create what they consider to be the best of times, defined according to a particular set of moral standards. Liberals and social democrats, on the other hand, tend to look forward to better times to come, so they pay more attention to civil society as a vehicle for creating new solutions. The relative marginalization of theories of the public sphere is partly explained by the ascendancy of conservatives and conservative thinking in Western politics.

In their political role, voluntary associations are seen as a crucial counterweight to states and corporate power and an essential pillar of promoting transparency, accountability and other aspects of "good governance," the favorite term of foreign-aid donors in recent times. Especially where formal citizenship rights are not well entrenched, it is civil society that provides the channels through which most people can make their voices heard in government decision-making, protect and promote their civil and political rights, and strengthen their skills as future political leaders. Arguing from democratic theory, a strong civil society can prevent the agglomeration of power that threatens autonomy and choice, provide effective checks against the abuse of state authority, and protect a democratic public sphere in which citizens can debate the ends and means of governance. The role of NGOs and social movements in mobilizing opposition to authoritarian rule and supporting progress toward multi-party elections has been well documented in Africa, Eastern Europe, Latin America and the Middle East.[16] Since the early 1990s these functions have been extended to the global level, with NGO networks becoming increasingly influential in challenging the policies of the international financial institutions and establishing new norms of accountability. Civil society in this sense means "people power" writ large.

On the surface at least, these arguments provide powerful support for the associational view of civil society. It would be disingenuous, however, to argue that official support for civil society is based purely on the findings of research. The fact that such support is "good for business" is also important.[17] By this I don't mean the business sector (though recent moves by corporations to cozy up to NGOs is another illustration of this trend), but any attempt by official institutions to develop "legitimacy by association" with citizens' groups which enjoy much higher levels of public trust. Developing positive relationships with civil society groups has become an essential "pre-defense" against attacks from the same sector. Both the World Bank and the specialized agencies of the United Nations are opening their doors, slowly, to civil society groups in this fashion, and the political costs of retreating into the bunker would likely be considerable in terms of their public image and support. Such trends raise the dangers of co-optation, of course, especially when NGOs already worry that "support for civil society" means "privatization by stealth," signifying the use of voluntary associations as a smokescreen for state retrenchment and corporate interests.

Since 2004, there have been signs that these high levels of interest and support are waning, confirming Alan Wolfe's judgment that the "idea of civil society failed because it became too popular."[18] "Civil society is passé" was the conclusion of a senior German government official in private conversation recently: "it had its moment in the 1990s but now it's time to move on to something else."[19] Some of these critiques have been intelligent and helpful, reaffirming the practical value of voluntary associations but rejecting the "conceits of civil society," as Neera Chandoke puts it, referring to exaggerated notions of their political importance or their ability to replace the nation-state (a fantasy akin to "grasping at straws," according to David Rieff).[20] Others have been knee-jerk reactions to anti-globalization and pro-social justice protests such as the "battle of Seattle" in 2000 and, more recently, the Spanish "indignados" and the various manifestations of Occupy across the world. There are a number of reasons for this backlash, including fears from governments in the South that NGOs may be replacing the state without any legitimacy or accountability; confusion about "who belongs" in civil society after the al-Qaeda attacks on New York and Washington, DC, on September 11, 2001; concerns among trade unions that NGOs have hijacked the name and functions of civil society for a narrow set of interests; and well-publicized cases of corruption in major charities.[21] Overall, however, these criticisms are very helpful, since they remind us that civil society is, and should continue to be, the subject of debate, in part because any institution that grows in influence must also be subjected to external pressure for accountability. NGOs now constitute a "fifth estate," according to one worldwide opinion poll undertaken in 2002.[22]

It is no longer possible to regard civil society as the preserve of a subset of privileged individuals – the citizens of the Greek *polis*, white male property-owners in eighteenth-century Europe, or the West, the North or the South. The idea of civil society has spread across the world to become a powerful leitmotif in politics and practice, yet it remains dominated by a narrow and disputed interpretation of what civil society is and does, and this narrowness threatens to erode its potential as a force for positive social change. Preserving this potential requires a simultaneous broadening of the debate to include other, less dominant, perspectives, and a much greater specification of what each of these perspectives has to contribute to a clearer understanding overall. And the starting point in that process is to break apart the assumptions that underpin the orthodox interpretation of civil society as the world of associational life.

2
Civil Society as Associational Life

In the late thirteenth century, Marco Polo was struck by the vibrancy of associational life in the Chinese city of Hangzhou, "noted for its charitable institutions as for its pleasures."[1] Public hospitals, market associations, free cemeteries, cultural groups and homes for the elderly abounded. No doubt earlier explorers would have seen similar things on their travels, too, since associations like these have existed from at least the days of the pharaohs. Human beings (at least most of us) are social creatures, and joining groups that help us to resolve the problems of collective action, advance the causes we believe in, find more meaning and fulfillment in life, or simply have some fun is a universal part of human experience. A life lived without such opportunities would be severely – perhaps unremittingly – diminished. For some, voluntary association is the natural state of humankind, invested with almost spiritual significance. "Human beings," writes J. Ronald Engel, "are made for the life of free association, and that divine reality, the Holy Spirit, is manifest in all associations committed to the democratic pursuit of justice in the common life."[2] Such attitudes are especially common in the USA, where the health and vitality of associations are often taken – at least by Americans – as the "envy of the world."[3] It was Alexis de Tocqueville that started this romance on his travels to the USA in the 1830s. "Americans of all ages, conditions and dispositions," he declared in a now-famous passage from his book *Democracy in America*, "have a constant tendency to form associations."[4] Today, over 750,000 Americans are members of voluntary fire brigades, for example (constituting 69 percent of all firefighters in the country), something that is as quintessentially American as the bucket brigade and hand truck in centuries gone by though some way down from the levels of 1983.[5]

This love affair has stirred passions on all sides of the political spectrum. Conservatives see associations as vehicles for rebuilding traditional moral values, while progressives see them as vehicles for reinventing whole societies. Yet does this mean that voluntary action is always the best way to run a fire service or achieve social reform? As long ago as 1911, Max Weber warned against romanticizing the effects of associations in his address to a congress of sociologists in Frankfurt: "the man of today is without doubt an association man in an awful and never dreamed of degree," he said, citing the negative effects on political engagement of the singing societies that were proliferating across Germany at the time – a fascinating anticipation of contemporary critiques of those such as Robert Putnam who praise the positive civic and political effects of choirs.[6] Associations matter hugely and should be encouraged, but there is equal danger in expecting too much from associational life, as if it were a "magic bullet" for resolving the intractable social, economic and political problems surveyed in brief in chapter 1. Increasingly, it seems, voluntary associations are expected to organize social services, govern local communities, solve the unemployment problem, save the environment, and still have time left over for rebuilding the moral life of nations. "Don't ask us to carry more than our capacity and then blame failure on us," says the Peruvian NGO leader Mario Padron; "we can't carry the load."[7]

This chapter focuses on civil society as a *part* of society that is distinct from states and markets, the most common of the understandings in use today and the direct descendant of de Tocqueville's ideas about nineteenth-century America. Commonly referred to as the "third" or "non-profit" sector, civil society in this sense contains all associations and networks between the family and the state in which membership and activities are "voluntary," including NGOs of different kinds, labor unions, political parties, churches and other religious groups, professional and business associations, community and self-help groups, social movements and the independent media. This is the "space of uncoerced human association," in Michael Walzer's famous definition, "and also the set of relational networks – formed for the sake of family, faith, interest and ideology – that fill this space."[8] The word "voluntary" here needs a little explication, since many such associations are run by paid professionals as well as volunteers. The key criteria are, first, that membership is consensual rather than legally required (meaning that "exit is possible without loss of status or public rights or benefits"); and, second, that voluntaristic mechanisms are used to achieve the association's objectives – through dialogue, bargaining and negotiation instead of enforced compliance by governments or market incentives from firms.[9] Whether such associations attract at least some voluntary contributions of time and/or money is a useful additional test.

Is there an "associational revolution" at work in the world today?

Voluntary associations have existed in most parts of the world for hundreds of years. The rural peasants' cooperatives that sprang into action after the French Revolution, for example; the Young Men's Lyceum in Springfield, Illinois, where Abraham Lincoln first practiced his oratory in 1838; the nineteenth-century reform movements such as Araya Samaj that pre-dated mass political action in India; and – despite the risks involved – the many dissident groups that remained active in Eastern Europe throughout communist rule. Since the late 1980s, however, the expansion of some

forms of associational life has been so rapid and so global
that commentators have begun to talk of an "associational
revolution" or a "power shift" of potentially momentous significance.[10] Except in a small number of cases where authoritarian governments still block the development of voluntary
associations on principle – in Myanmar and Cuba, for example
– the numbers of registered non-profit organizations have
increased at rates not seen before in history, especially in
developing countries, which started from a lower base and
have received large amounts of foreign aid for investment in
NGOs.

For example, India had 3.3 million NGOs in 2009, up from
approximately one million fifteen years earlier, while Brazil
counted 220,000 and Egypt over 24,000 in 2007.[11] In Ghana,
Zimbabwe and Kenya, the sector provides 40 percent or
more of all healthcare and education services delivered. And
even in China, where government policy remains suspicious,
the number of registered national non-profit organizations
had already reached 2,000 by 2001.[12] Paralleling this increase
in numbers has been the growth of individual NGOs to cover
the provision of services to large sections of the population,
especially in South Asia – over 113 million people in the
case of the Bangladesh Rural Advancement Committee, for
example, in 2012.[13]

In Western Europe and the USA, such steep growth rates
are less evident but the overall totals of voluntary associations are still impressive. There are approximately 1.5 million
registered charities in the USA for example, and at least
164,000 in the UK, plus another 600,000 "informal" groups.[14]
However, these figures disguise important shifts in the composition of associational life. In both the UK and the USA,
religious groups and formally registered "intermediary" NGOs
have grown since the late 1980s while non-religious membership groups and labor unions have declined, though there
has recently been a resurgence in grassroots action among
low-income and immigrant communities that holds great
promise for the future.[15] This decline has been especially
acute in the labor movement, with unions in the USA

representing only one-third of the workers they represented
in the early 1950s,[16] and among what Theda Skocpol calls
"locally rooted but nationally active" cross-class membership
associations such as the American Legion and the AFL-CIO
(the umbrella movement for the US labor movement).
Skocpol concludes that, as a consequence, US civil society
has moved "from membership to management."[17] In other
words, the traditional Tocquevillian core of associational life
is being rapidly eroded. This decline seems especially acute
among women, perhaps because of increasing demands on
their time and the inadequacy of childcare support in
America. Where such support is available (for example in
the UK, Canada and the Netherlands), the impact on women's
participation in voluntary associations is highly positive.[18]
Overall, then, the numbers of voluntary associations in the
United States and the UK are stable or increasing slowly in
quantitative terms, but this trend masks important variations
in *who* participates in *what*.

At the international level, a new layer of NGOs and NGO
networks has emerged since the early 1990s to constitute a
"global civil society," at least in some interpretations. Over
56,000 international NGOs and 25,000 transnational NGO
networks are already active on the world stage, 90 percent
of which have been formed since 1970.[19] They include
famous names such as Oxfam and Save the Children, campaigns such as those on land mines and arms control, global
movements such as the Hemispheric Social Alliance (which
already claims to have 49 million members), federations of
community groups such as Shack Dwellers International
linking hundreds of thousands of people across three conti-
nents, and international associations of mayors, local authorities, business representatives, professionals, universities and
writers.

However, despite this avalanche of figures, we are left with
only one unambiguous fact about trends in associational life
worldwide: the numbers of formally registered NGOs have
risen substantially since 1989. What this trend *means* for civil
society is unclear. Because the data for most of the world

cover only registered organizations, trends in other areas of associational life are difficult to identify, especially those below the radar of academic research such as community groups and grassroots movements. We do not know whether past developments are a reliable guide to the future (especially once NGOs are forced to rely on money raised from their own societies, not from foreign aid), and scholars cannot agree on what the broader implications of these trends might be. An "associational revolution" or "power shift" would surely signal structural changes in politics, economics and social relations, not just an increase in the numbers and size of NGOs at work on the margins. In any case, it makes no sense to lump all non-profit organizations into a single category of "associational life," from the Ford Foundation to a burial society in South Africa, or to fixate – as the foreign-aid community has done – on NGOs as the most important type of association among so many. The first source of disagreement concerns the thorny issue of which associations belong in civil society, and which do not.

Who is "in" and who is "out"?

The three-sector model of society implies that states, markets and non-profit groups are separate from and independent of each other – hermetically sealed, perhaps, in their own rationalities and particular ways of working. Yet even a glance at real institutions demonstrates that this is nonsense. Boundaries are always fluid, and there are reasons why this is necessarily so. I, like you, am simultaneously citizen, neighbor, voter, worker and consumer, and the qualities developed in one of these roles spill over into the others, one hopes with positive effects. Civil society and the state, for example, have always been interdependent, with states providing the legal and regulatory framework a democratic civil society needs to function, and civil society exerting the pressure for accountability that keeps elected governments on track. As Skocpol has shown, effective US social policies between 1945 and

1980 worked through symbiotic ties that developed between government and locally rooted membership associations.[20] This does not mean, of course, that civil society is part of the state or vice versa – they are clearly different sets of institutions – but if they are disconnected then the positive effects of each on the other can be negated. Whether states have more influence over civil society or civil societies over states has been a source of disagreement among scholars for two hundred years or more, but clearly government policy can have a major impact on the strength and shape of associational life – think of attacks on the labor movement or, in more positive vein, the encouragement of non-profit-sector service provision under governments of both parties in the UK and USA. However, if these links become too close and cozy, then governments can be captured by particular interests in civil society, and civil society cannot play its watchdog role on government. State institutions, therefore, cannot be part of associational life.

Sitting between associations and the state, however, is a gray area called "political society" consisting of parties, political organizations and parliaments that has divided civil society scholars into two rival camps. The first camp sees political society as a crucial component of civil society, not because civic groups seek state power (they don't) or because they aggregate the interests of individuals into political settlements (they can't), but because they generate influence on politics through the life of democratic associations and unconstrained discussion in the public sphere. "In the long run, democratic political societies depend for their health on the depth of their roots in independent pre-political associations and publics."[21] Solidarity in Poland was both a labor union and a political party in waiting, and social movements usually have implicit political agendas. In Rajasthan, for example, the Mazdoor Kisan Shakti Sangathan, a "non-party political formation" that works with workers' and peasants' groups, has already fielded candidates in local elections and is considering entering the race for office at the state level too.[22] In countries such as Indonesia with weak multi-party systems (or where parties are forbidden at the local level), alliances between national political formations on the one hand, and peasant movements and labor unions at the local and regional levels on the other, are developing rapidly.[23] Examples like these, in which groups are simultaneously involved in mobilizing popular participation and linking to branches of the state that foster and draw on them for different tasks, are especially common in societies undergoing democratization, mirroring the experience of neighborhood committees in Taiwan, Singapore and South Korea in the 1970s and 1980s. Such links make open protest risky, but maintain space for less confrontational strategies and tactics.[24] South Africa's Treatment Action Campaign began as an alliance of NGOs determined to change government policy on retroviral drugs for HIV/AIDS patients, but is now developing some of the characteristics of an opposition against the background of rule by the African National Congress, though without a formal political identity. And leaders in countries such as Chile, the Philippines and Brazil move regularly from NGOs to government and back.[25] Overall, then, linkages between civil and political society are natural, useful and to be encouraged, especially at a time when the balance between direct and representative democracy is changing in favor of the former.

The second camp shudders at the corrupting influence of politics on associations, since associations are assumed to be independent of any partisan political interests. If they weren't independent, they wouldn't be able to play the role that is claimed for them in cementing generalized trust and tolerance across different political communities and promoting a genuine sense of the common or public interest. Neo-Tocquevillian thinkers accept that apolitical associations can have political effects because of their influence on overall levels of political participation, including voting, though the evidence for and against this proposition is contested.[26] However, this is not the same as formal political activity, and there are certainly examples of the damage that can be done when voluntary associations formally ally themselves with parties competing for votes. ADAB (the association of NGOs in Bangladesh), for example, joined forces with the Awami League in 1996, leading to new forms of patron–client relationships once the league had been elected into office.[27] Ten years later, the Nobel Peace Prize winner Muhammad Yunus tried to start a new political party in Bangladesh called Citizens' Power, but found that even the deep networks of the Grameen Bank and other successful NGOs could not make inroads into the political establishment.[28] In the USA, religious conservatives (through the Christian Coalition of America) have regularly used their connections with senior Republicans in Washington, DC, to influence public policy on reproductive rights and other issues. Of course, similar examples could be cited from the Democrats, but that is not my point – any association that claims to promote the public interest is in dangerous water when it allies itself with a partisan political agenda, since it forfeits its claim to represent the broader agenda of civil society. "We're sick of politics" is a familiar refrain among community groups and volunteers. For many, while trust is the lubricant of civil society, hypocrisy is the Vaseline of political influence.

There has always been a strong strain of "antipolitics," as György Konrád (1989) calls it, among civil society enthusiasts, driven partly by the belief that civil society can organize and govern itself successfully without the need for government intervention, or for government at all in the conventional sense of the word. This may be true at the scale of a New England town meeting, but it is unlikely to be effective at the national level, and even less in global regimes, despite the increasing importance of direct democracy in filling out the processes of politics. So, while the state is definitely "out" of civil society and non-partisan political activity is definitely "in," everything between these two extremes remains an object of dispute. The only acceptable compromise seems to be that political parties are *in* civil society when they are out of office and *out* of civil society when they are in.

In case the situation is not sufficiently muddy, the boundary between civil society and the market is even less clear.

Here again there is disagreement between those who fear for the purity of the civic spirit when contaminated by contact with business, and those such as Ernest Gellner (1994) who argue that business is inescapably a part of civil society, or at least the private-property relations and market institutions that business needs to flourish. Going back at least to the writings of John Locke, this strand of theory has always seen private economic activity as a crucial mainstay of civil society because, at least in theory, it diffuses power away from states and helps to protect the freedom of individuals. This tradition is echoed today in the increasing use of non-profit agencies in the provision of social and economic services and the rise of "philanthrocapitalism" that is analyzed in chapter 3 – the increasing adoption of business thinking and market mechanisms by charities and foundations.[29] Critics of this tradition see civil society as a social, cultural and political phenomenon, consigning service providers to the not-for-profit sector of the marketplace and insisting on the independence of citizens' groups from economic interests. Both Michael Walzer and Christopher Lasch insist that civil society is a sphere of life – a market-free zone – in which "money is devalued," while Cohen and Arato conclude that "only a concept of civil society differentiated from the economy . . . can become the center of a critical social and political theory."[30] In practice, however, it is difficult to draw these distinctions in such a watertight manner. It was the market women of Sierra Leone, for example, who (acting collectively) thronged the streets of Freetown in 1996 and again in 1997 to ensure that democratic elections went ahead. Likewise, Ashutosh Varshney's research has shown that business associations that tie together the economic interests of Hindus and Muslims in Indian cities have been crucial in reducing the incidence of intercommunal violence (or exacerbating it where they are absent). And, in Cuba, it is small-scale, informal enterprises that provide some space for independent organization where other forms of association are controlled by the state.[31]

This confusion is partly due to a failure to specify what kind of "business" is being talked about. The institutional and legally mandated aims of a multinational corporation such as Shell or IBM, for example, are different to those of sections of the business community that exist, at least in part, to generate a social good or advance a collective interest, such as cooperatives, credit unions, social enterprises and public–private partnerships. In developing societies, where the formal sector of the economy is often very small, most economic activity takes place anyway in the informal sector, where social relations and market relations are inextricably inter-woven. One also needs to distinguish between profit-seeking activities by individual enterprises and the civic or political role of business associations – such as the Transatlantic Business Dialogue or a national chamber of commerce. Logically, the former would be excluded from civil society but the latter would not. Such associations could have an important role to play in encouraging attitudes of cooperation and trust, as well as representing the interests of their members.

The most difficult and contested question about "who is in and who is out" revolves around the definition of "civil" and "uncivil" society, a debate explored in chapter 3 because it concerns the nature of the good society, the role of the family and much else besides, not simply the characteristics of associations. But it is worth mentioning that models of associational life find it difficult to exclude any non-state or non-market institution so long as they meet the structural or analytical criteria for membership described above. Of course, some writers do exclude associations of which they disapprove, but not on any grounds that can be defended without considerable intellectual gymnastics and the imposi-tion of a particular – and therefore partial – definition of the good, the bad and the ugly. In my view, structural models of civil society hold water only if all non-coercive associations are included. Hence, although the boundaries between vol-untary associations, states and markets are increasingly fluid they are not disappearing: Oxfam is not Shell, and Occupy is not the US government (at least not yet).

Organizations and ecosystems

Neo-Tocquevillians often focus on non-profit organizations or the "non-profit sector," which is a subset of associational life as a whole – the "peaks above the waterline" as opposed to the "iceberg" of citizen action underneath, which is organized less formally through grassroots groups and membership associations of many different kinds.[32] More useful, in my view, is to take a systems view of associational life that looks at the different components of civil society and how they interact. Like a complex and fragile ecosystem, civil society gains strength when grassroots groups, non-profit intermediaries and membership associations are linked together in ways that promote collective goals, cross-society coalitions, mutual accountability and shared action-learning. This is one generalization that does hold up across many different contexts: "the landscape of the third sector is untidy but wonderfully exuberant . . . what counts is not the confusion but the profusion."[33] Associations promote pluralism by enabling multiple interests to be represented, different functions to be performed and a wide range of capacities to be developed. No one set of organizations could hope to cover more than a small subsection of these roles, capacities and interests, so pluralism *within* civil society is essential.

Drawing from social capital theory, this means a balance between "bonding" (connections within groups), "bridging" (connections across them) and "linking" (connections between associations, government and the market). Bonding may accentuate inequalities since associations will be used to promote the interests only of the groups concerned, and this can lead to gridlock in the system as a result of special-interest politics. Bridging should reduce them over time as people dissolve their differences in a sense of the wider common interest, and linking should help all groups to prosper by making the right connections with institutions that can offer them support, resources, opportunities and influence.[34] However, without the security provided by strong in-group ties, bridging may expose those on the margins to environments in which they cannot compete on equal terms, or benefit the few that can prosper at the expense of the many who are left behind.

Strongly bonded associations (such as community organizations) are more effective when they link together vertically and horizontally to form both cross-cutting networks and federations that can take the struggle to the next level, and alliances across the lines of class, race and religion that build from a strong grassroots base. "Just as life assembles itself into chains, nonprofits aggregate either by linking up interests, people or communities, or by linking to related organizations," concludes Paul Hawken in his study of the worldwide environmental movement.[35] The Pushback Network, Gamaliel and the Industrial Areas Foundation in the USA are other good examples, as are the peasant federations studied by Tony Bebbington that connect small-producer groups together in Latin America.[36] But non-profit intermediaries or NGOs are also important, supplying much of the "connective tissue" of civil society by providing specialist support, capacity-building and advocacy services to broader networks and alliances. SPARC, an NGO in Mumbai, has developed a worldwide reputation for this kind of role in support of the Shack Dwellers International movement.

When civil society networks join forces on a scale and over a time-span significant enough to force through more fundamental change, they can be classified as social movements. Successful social movements (think civil rights in the USA, the movement of the landless in Brazil, and the environmental and women's movements worldwide) tend to have three things in common – a powerful idea, ideal or policy agenda; effective communications strategies to get these ideas into politics, government and the media; and a strong constituency or social base that provides the muscle required to make those targets listen and ensure that constituency views are accurately represented.[37] When these three things come together, success is possible even when the odds are stacked against them. In the USA, for example, the Living Wage Campaign succeeded in getting legislation adopted in a number of states and cities despite a conservative Congress during the 2000s, while STISSS, the healthcare workers' union in El Salvador, persuaded government to outlaw the privatization of healthcare because of its effects in excluding the poor.[38] Of course, movements are not always progressive in their politics. One of the most successful in America since the early 1980s has been the rise of neo-conservatism, anchored in the associations of the religious right (for example, the Promise Keepers and the Moral Majority), but well connected both to think-tanks – such as the Heritage Institute – and to the Republican Party.[39] The Tea Party, another element of this movement that was launched in 2009, is often derided by progressives, but research shows that it has some real support at the grassroots level and a strong binding ideology as well as funding from conservative philanthropists and a regular supply of ideas from think-tanks and lobby groups.[40] Indeed, the Tea Party's ideological mirror image in the form of Occupy and other protests against tax evasion in the USA and UK that erupted in 2011 have more in common with conservative movements than their protagonists might admit. Both grew from a sense of widespread frustration with the status quo and implied a rebellion against authority, and like other social movements or episodes of movement-like activity before them they continue to wax and wane. Contrary to some popular interpretations of its importance at the time, Occupy has not "changed everything,"[41] for this is not how most social movements work. History shows that they are most effective in the long term when they are anchored in a broader repertoire of contentious politics that connects them to their targets and their allies over time.[42]

As in a real ecosystem, all parts need to be present and connected if the system is to operate effectively. Remove or weaken one part, or strengthen others artificially, and the system breaks down. An insufficient density, diversity or depth of associations leaves societies more vulnerable to authoritarian rule because the ecosystem cannot withstand external shocks. For example, if only one independent newspaper or watchdog organization exists, governments can easily throttle dissent (think of Zimbabwe under Robert Mugabe), but if thirty exist, at least some will survive (think of Uganda or even China). Worst of all is homogeneity, the Achilles' heel of ecosystems both natural and social. Yet real associational ecosystems are replete with gaps, weaknesses and donor-led conformity. Informal associations at the grass-roots are often ignored or neglected, but they were vital to the struggle, for example, against apartheid in South Africa or for democracy in China today – organizations such as yard and street resident committees, burial and temple societies, farmers' associations and youth clubs. At the same time, new kinds of civil society associations have emerged, often organized horizontally instead of vertically, without the bureaucratic or democratic structures that characterized their forebears and making much more use of social media. In the USA they include groups that help to organize restaurant workers, domestic workers and others, but not as part of the formal labor movement.[43] The impact of these new associations is considered in chapter 5.

Even if one rejects the thesis that civil society is in decline because of these changes, it is impossible to ignore the fact that its shape is changing in important ways in every part of the world. This is to be expected, since associational life is never static, but, if concentrated power is bad for democracy in general, it is difficult to argue that it is good for civil society, yet some of these changes have come dangerously close to this effect. There has been a worldwide professionalization of the non-profit sector in a technocratic sense, and a gradual distancing of associations from their social base – what has been variously described as "NGO-ization," "corporatization" and the rise of the "Non-Profit Industrial Complex."[44] Funding has gone overwhelmingly to larger NGOs, well-known think-tanks, and advocacy groups in capital cities, while Northern NGOs have dominated the emergence of transnational networks. This is not strengthening civil society, but promoting certain associations over others on the basis of preconceived notions of how civil society should operate, and it creates widening divisions between different elements in the ecosystem. Increasingly, one might say, NGOs are traveling in business class while the rest of civil society stays behind in coach, both literally and metaphorically. Yet even these observations are dependent on the context in which they are made. The associational ecosystem may look and behave very differently from one society to another.

Associational life in cross-cultural perspective

Civil society theory, for the most part, has been developed in Europe and the USA and it makes a series of assumptions about the characteristics of voluntary associations that may not travel well across countries, cultures and different periods in time. They may not even be accurate for different communities within the same country – African-American associational life in America, for example, or Islamic associations in England, or groups led by women rather than by men. Norms of participation are different among whites and African-Americans in the USA, with the latter more likely to take part in protest and campaigning activities as part of an oppositional culture that characterizes many of their associations.[45] Confucian cultures think differently about belonging, solidarity and citizenship, in part because of a stress on the collective rather than the individual. Social memberships – at least historically – were non-optional and priority was given to the needs of the social whole, so it is no surprise that associations in countries like China have always found it difficult to exist outside of government control.[46] Similarly, Islam's communal character necessitates that the autonomy of individuals must sometimes give way to the needs of the broader community, but also that all ethical questions must be constantly re-evaluated by that community as well.[47] The reality of associational life in non-Western cultures is always one of "mix and match" because they have been subject to so many external influences in both the colonial and postcolonial eras. To enlarge on this point it may be useful to look at the combination of associational cultures in more detail in two regions that are of particular interest to civil society watchers: the Middle East and Africa.

Associational life in the Middle East

Most famously for Ernest Gellner, civil society cannot exist in non-Western societies since it is the product of a specific period in the evolution of the West. Gellner refused to believe that regions like the Middle East with strong Islamic traditions could ever develop a meaningful civic life, because Islam as an institution cannot be left and entered freely. "You can join the Labour Party without slaughtering a sheep," as he once remarked, "and leave it without incurring the death penalty for apostasy."[48] As recent events have shown, however, such judgments are far too crude to provide an accurate guide to the diverse realities of associational life in Middle Eastern societies, where many different kinds of Islamic organization coexist, cooperate and compete with secular NGOs, think-tanks, women's groups, protest movements, labor unions, media outlets and bloggers. The resulting mix changes markedly from one country to another, so associational life in Oman or Libya is very different to that in Jordan, Egypt or Kuwait. One of the most important aspects of the vibrant contemporary debate about civil society in the Muslim world is the conscious rejection of imposed Western models, and the "clash of civilizations" thesis that sometimes accompanies them, in favor of a much more nuanced exploration of how patterns of associational life are taking shape on the ground in different contexts. The focus of attention is on actualizing forms of civic and democratic behavior that are feasible under different political regimes.

When a college-educated Tunisian street vendor named Mohamed Bouazizi set fire to himself in a protest over political and economic conditions in 2011, he set in motion a train of events that challenged Gellner's hypothesis as it had not been challenged before. Variously described as the "Arab Spring," the "Arab Awakening" and the "Arab Intifada," the large-scale popular protests that spread rapidly across the region after this event seemed to signify a watershed for civil society in the region. As of 2013, and in common with previous experiences of civil society uprisings in Eastern Europe and elsewhere, this sense of euphoria has been harshly tempered, but it has not disappeared. The path to democracy rarely leads directly from the streets to the offices of the state. Yet the condition of associational life in the Middle East will surely never be the same.

The Arab Spring did not, however, spring from nowhere. Nor was it launched spontaneously by social media, though the occupation of Cairo's Tahrir Square and other iconic public spaces did unfold without much warning or formal preparation.[49] Its origins lie much further back in the history of associational life in the region, through a wide variety of groups whose activities in neighborhoods, factories, mosques and universities helped to underpin the eventual emergence of large-scale protest.[50] Recent scholarship has shown that elements of voluntarism existed even in traditional Islamic associations such as guilds (or *asnaf*), trusts and foundations funded by endowments (called *waqfs*), charities funded through tithes, or *zakat*, and *ayan*, or groups of "urban notables." These groups coexisted with tribal institutions, merchants' groups, labor unions, secular organizations of intellectuals, and professional associations before the repression of civic activity by post-independence governments in the Arab world who sought to consolidate their newfound power in the face of what some saw as threats to national unity.[51] Beginning in the 1980s, these patterns began to open up in response to economic liberalization (which created space for service-providing NGOs), limited political reforms and the spread of Islamist movements.

In Egypt, for example, pro-democracy movements like Kefaya (Arabic for "Enough") and the Movement to Reclaim University Independence began to emerge in response to these openings in the mid-2000s. They were joined by groups of strikers (especially textile workers) who distanced themselves from the official labor movement, networks of blogger activists,[52] and emboldened civil society groups such as Writers and Artists for Change and Egyptians against Torture, which was organized to confront the excesses of the state security apparatus.[53] In Egypt and across the Middle East, associational life developed a fascinating mixture of the secular and the religious, the traditional and the modern, co-optation, independence and all shades in between.[54] In Turkey, for example, independent associations of urban working women with freely chosen memberships coexist with Islamic associations that are closed to other faiths, while in Jordan and Morocco, students' organizations, youth and women's groups and proto-social movements are beginning to influence mainstream Muslim discourse. At the opposite end of the political spectrum (in countries such as Saudi Arabia, Qatar and the United Arab Emirates) independent citizens' organizations are prohibited and state-run "NGOs" are the norm, along with semi-official Islamic charities (called *diwaniyyas*) and quasi-official research institutes and think-tanks.

In these authoritarian contexts there is little prospect that associational life is about to flourish, but in the countries affected by the Arab Spring it will be very difficult to close off all routes to protest and participation. The question that then presents itself is clear: how will different kinds of civil society associations take advantage of the spaces that emerge? Despite the diversity of associational life in the region, it is Islamist movements that tend to dominate debates about the answers to this question, especially those that have achieved electoral success such as Hamas, Hezbollah and the Muslim Brotherhood in Egypt. Such movements are themselves diverse, of course, but most combine the need to engage in democratic politics in order to gain political power, with the continuation of anti-democratic sentiments once they have it. Relationships between these groups and other voluntary associations in the Middle East are obviously tense because they involve contests over ideology, profile and power, but given the strong ties that Islamists enjoy with large grassroots constituencies and the elite-based nature of many NGOs and advocacy groups (often dependent on funding from outside their own societies), such movements offer a natural vehicle for politics and the development of the social mores governing political and economic life. Islamists enjoy the popular support and legitimacy required to challenge the moral and political authority of incumbent regimes, while NGOs (even if externally funded and restricted in their roles) have a presence at both grassroots and international levels that can pull in new ideas and resources, and develop skills and capacities that may eventually translate into change higher up the system. But huge gaps and disconnects remain in the civil society ecosystem, requiring long-term support to encourage these different interests to engage with each other over time. Through that process, there might yet be a democratic resolution of the ongoing "internal struggle over who gets to define the Islamic reformation that is already underway in most of the Muslim world."[55] "The Arab Awakening is going to be measured in decades, not months or years," writes Marwan Muasher; "we are going to experience many springs, summers, falls and winters."[56]

That struggle includes liberal NGO activists, feminist leaders, moderate Islamists, "repentant Jihadists" (former Islamic militants who have won release from prison by renouncing violence) and scholars such as Adullahi An-Na'im, who are developing new visions of civil and political life rooted firmly in the Islamic tradition *and* explicitly committed to equal citizenship and respect for human rights, under a democratic, secular state.[57] There are certainly problems with associational life in the Middle East – as shown by the continued intransigence of governments both old and new in the face of the Arab Spring – but this is not because civil society is "un-Islamic." "The compatibility or incompatibility of Islam and democracy is not a matter of philosophical speculation but of political struggle," concludes Asef Bayat, which is why the evolution of locally rooted visions of associational life holds some of the keys to the future of the Muslim world.[58]

Associational life in Africa

Early work on civil society in Africa tended to deny the applicability of the concept completely or look for patterns of associational life that replicated those familiar from the West. Neither approach proved convincing, and today there is renewed interest in creating civil society theories and practices with distinctively African flavors. The starting point in this effort is to recognize the impact of colonialism on the ways in which different forms of associational life were categorized and dealt with by the colonial authorities. As Mahmood Mamdani has shown using examples from South Africa and Uganda, the bifurcation of British rule into indirect authority exercised through customary law in rural areas, and direct authority exercised through civil law in urban centers, had important consequences for civil society and governance that still reverberate today. One of these consequences has been an ongoing debate between "liberal modernists and Africanist communitarians" about the relative importance of "modern" (urban) and "traditional" (rural) associations that reflects this historical divide. Mamdani's solution to the "impasse" he sees in this debate is to call for a creative fusion of elements from both "civil society and community" into new ecosystems of associational life that are more deeply rooted in African societies, and hence, one hopes, more effective in fulfilling their various roles.[59]

It is important to note that the bifurcation of civil and customary authority was a deliberate strategy to consolidate colonial rule, but it also over-emphasized the differences between urban and rural, modern and traditional forms of governance and association. Social structures based on tribe and clan are characteristic of African societies, and they have given rise to strong ascriptive associations based on ethnicity in which membership is inherited, as opposed to voluntary in the sense implied by Western civil society theory. But excluding them from civil society makes no sense when they occupy such an important position in the fabric of associational life, and in which they organize many forms of collective action from mutual aid to informal debate and decision-making. In Uganda, Ghana and Nigeria, ethnicity has provided a focus for popular mobilization in contexts where existing power arrangements have closed down other routes to participation in democratic governance. Of course it has also been used to mobilize violence and dispossession in recent electoral competitions in Kenya and elsewhere, but often what appear as ethnic conflicts are more straightforward struggles over access to power and resources that are manipulated along clan or tribal lines.[60]

Even in colonial Africa a wide variety of different associations coexisted. Nationalist movements emerged alongside independent churches, women's and self-help groups, professional and neighborhood associations, credit and burial societies, labor unions, farmers' organizations and politico-cultural networks. These associations were spurred on by urbanization and rural–urban migration, increasing access to education, and the development of the market economy (which both required and created an increasing range of intermediaries, mutual-support and interest-based associations); by the struggle for independence, in which civil society activists often played key roles (especially in Southern Africa); and by the trend toward decentralization and democracy in the post-independence era, when advocacy, development and human rights NGOs began to emerge across the continent.[61] During the 1980s, the flowering of democracy in Eastern Europe and rising controversy over economic policies such as "structural adjustment" gave new impetus to NGOs and community organizations such as these, which also received increasing amounts of foreign aid in an effort to ensure greater accountability from newly elected governments, to provide additional routes to citizen participation where representative political systems fell short, and to deliver development-related services to low-income and other marginalized populations. As in the Middle East, associational life in Africa became increasingly diverse, but in the minds of donor agencies only NGOs appeared to count.

The debate alluded to by Mamdani has been brought into sharper focus by recent criticisms of NGOs in Africa which are largely urban-based but have little connection to a domestic constituency or supporter base, raising question marks about their legitimacy and sustainability, and their ability to lever changes in politics, the economy and power. On the other hand, strongly rooted associations that are often organized around ethnicity may face difficulties in building relationships across different groups, which tend to be important in consolidating a democratic political culture. This is one reason why broad-based civic action in Africa is quite rare, often emerging only at times of crisis and difficult to sustain beyond the first or second wave of democratic elections – even in South Africa, where NGOs and community-based organizations were so influential prior to and after the end of apartheid and now number over 50,000 strong, or in Kenya, which has three times that number of associations.[62]

What is intriguing in this picture is not whether "modern" NGOs or "traditional" community associations are more authentic or effective than the other, but how these different elements are going to intertwine so that the "whole" of associational life "is more than the sum of its parts," since this is the only way in which the ecosystem will be able to influence the larger questions of politics and democracy. Clearly, there are factors other than the structure of associational life that are important in this respect, principally the nature of contemporary political regimes. In most African countries these regimes continue to restrict the ability of anyone in civil society to influence public affairs, regardless of the kind of associations to which they belong. As David Sogge puts it,

> where Africans could organize to transform the political order ... rights and collective self-esteem have advanced. Yet where the interplay of global interests and national vulnerabilities

has had the upper hand the advance of citizenship has been halted or reversed . . . African leaders have squandered public goods and public trust. Political competition and space for active citizenship have been marginalized or pushed underground.[63]

And infiltration or even direct control of civil society associations by the state is common in countries such as Cameroon, Benin, Ethiopia and Sudan.[64] The inability or unwillingness of governments to create inclusive institutions and act in the long-term interests of society as a whole has undermined development in Africa when compared to the success of countries like South Korea and Taiwan.

In resolving this situation, the key question is not "does civil society exist in Africa?" (it does), but "what are different African associations doing?" and "how can we help them to achieve more going forward, alone and together, in ways that are adapted to and effective in different local contexts?" The reality (in Africa as elsewhere) is that people draw on a wide range of cultural resources and identities in their associational involvements, be they modern, traditional or somewhere in between. The debate highlighted by Mamdani may never be settled because civil society is continuously evolving, but moving "beyond the backlash" against both African NGOs and customary associations will help us to understand and encourage the different ways in which the ecosystems of associational life are evolving across the continent.[65]

Far from being a problem, the diverse development of these ecosystems across Africa, the Middle East and other regions is a cause for celebration, because it means that what emerges in the future – hybrid, fluid and maybe surprising to commentators in the West – might be able to avoid some of the problems encountered elsewhere. This may help to answer the charge that NGOs and other associations in these regions are simply pawns of foreign powers. Associational life in every country is a process of mix and match, with lots of different elements recombining over time. The consequences of this process are always uncertain, particularly in contexts where radically different cultures of identity and belonging coexist. That is why no simple relationships exist between the forms, norms and achievements of voluntary associations. But if that is the case, how is civil society as the good society to be created?

3
Civil Society as the Good Society

When the Egyptian scholar–activist Saad Eddin Ibrahim stood up to defend himself in front of the Supreme State Security Court in Cairo one July day in 2002, he focused on one key phrase, "civil society," by which he meant a society where all could be free to speak their minds and have their voices heard.[1] Although accused on spurious grounds of financial mismanagement as the head of a prominent Egyptian NGO, the Ibn Khaldoun Centre, Ibrahim was arrested because he – and by extension "civil society" – was perceived to pose a threat to the reigning political order. Not many of us would be as brave or as principled as this, but all of us carry in our hearts and minds a vision of the world as we would want it to be – ruled, at the most general level, by love and forgiveness, truth and beauty, courage and compassion. Even in an age obsessed by terrorism, mercifully few people wake up each morning to plan the final details of an attack on the World Trade Center or the Federal Building in Oklahoma City, select their targets for a killing spree at the local high school, or identify which of their opponents are next in line for ethnic cleansing. Of course, the details of the good society are subject to a never-ending debate about ends and means, necessary compromises and trade-offs between different interests and objectives, but the idea of the good society remains a driving force behind the best of contemporary politics and collective action. Increasingly, "civil society" is used as shorthand for the kind of society in which we want to live.

The use of civil society as a metaphor for the good society has its roots in the Greek *polis* and the "commonwealths" described in chapter 1, in religious doctrines about spiritual communities such as the Islamic *ummah* or the Jewish *tikkun olam*, and in Kantian thinking about a global ethical community or the *civitas humana* of William Roepke and other conservatives.[2] In its now dominant liberal-democratic form it was the inspiration for dissident groups in Eastern Europe and the former Soviet Union during the 1980s, where it symbolized a call to "institutionalize the principles of citizenship on which modern liberal, democratic politics are based" and became almost a synonym – or "shining emblem" – for democracy, freedom and even "decency" in general.[3] For Vaclav Havel, ex-president of Czechoslovakia, "civic society" was "the social order towards which all modern democratic societies are gradually working," while Victor Perez-Diaz made a similar argument for the "return of civil society" in Spain after the end of General Franco's regime.[4] Since 1989 these ideas have been detached somewhat from their liberal-democratic moorings and taken up by a wider range of ideological and cultural positions, including the global justice movement on the left (mobilized at the World Social Forum under the slogan "another world is possible"), scholars arguing against self-interest as the basis for social science and public policy, feminists searching for a rationality not based on "economic man," opposition movements in many countries, and those who see in Islamic civil society the roots of a "civilized life" that is different from the West. In Bengali, "civil society" (or *shushil shamaj*) is often translated as "gentle society," while in Turkey it refers to "that which is not related to the military."[5]

Not all of these positions use the precise phrase "civil society," but they do share an image of civil society as a desirable social order or self-image of modernity defined in normative terms. Although these norms sometimes differ, tolerance, non-discrimination, non-violence, trust and cooperation are common denominators, along with freedom and democracy so long as these are not defined exclusively in Western terms – freedom from want being as important as freedom from arbitrary government intervention, and democracy being valued in the marketplace and global governance as well as in domestic politics. In this sense, civil society represents the institutionalization of "civility" as a different way of living in the world. Too many of our existing social, economic and political systems destroy the bonds we want to have with each other and with the natural world that surrounds us, and civil society seems to offer a way of reconstituting these relationships on the basis of a different set of values in a rapidly changing global context. Elsewhere I have analyzed civil society as "the marriage of love and reason," each essential in and of itself and as a counterweight to the other.[6] This philosophy, with its roots deep in Gandhian ethics and the teachings of Martin Luther King, sees personal and social transformation as mutually supportive, and unconditional love (the ultimate extension of civility, one might say) as a potentially revolutionary force in the public sphere, not just in our private lives. Marrying a rich inner life dedicated to the cultivation of loving kindness and compassion with the practice of new forms of politics, economics and public policy is the key to social transformation. According to Aung Sang Suu Kyi, the Burmese activist and politician, "Without a revolution of the spirit, the forces which produced the iniquities of the old order would continue to be operative, posing a constant threat to the process of reform and regeneration."[7]

At the transnational level, these ideas are reflected in the rising popularity of "global civil society," not as the additional layer of associational life described in chapter 2, but as a mechanism by which new global norms are developed and cemented around notions of universal human rights, international cooperation and the peaceful resolution of our differences. George Soros's "global open society," Richard Falk's "humane governance," David Held's "cosmopolitan democracy," the "global civil society" of John Keane and Mary Kaldor, my own "future positive," and the "global ethical community" of even a philosopher as gloomy as Peter Singer all represent versions of this same idea, despite the fact that we are at least a generation away from any kind of cosmopolitan democracy or "cosmocracy." We will look at these claims more closely in chapter 5. Paul Hawken views current developments in the environmental movement as comparable to the "Axial Age" between 900 and 200 BC, when many religious traditions emerged around versions of the "Golden Rule," and from which – however imperfectly – a different set of values began to permeate across the world.[8]

Civil society associations that work for greater equity and justice do see the structure, culture and achievements of civil society as intimately related to each other. CIVICUS, for example (the "World Alliance for Citizen Participation"), has developed a whole methodology for measuring the strength of civil society on all three dimensions, with norms and values at the center.[9] There is, however, an important difference between "a society that is civil" because it possesses high levels of generalized trust and cooperation (or "social capital," to use a now conventional shorthand) and one that is "civil" because it succeeds in solving particular public-policy dilemmas in ways that are just and effective. Some civil society enthusiasts (especially the neo-Tocquevillians) might argue that these two understandings are the same, since such generalized norms – anchored in a healthy associational life – will facilitate effective public-policy-making as people of goodwill come to a fair and sensible consensus over matters of pressing concern. But in the analysis that follows it is important to keep them separate, for two interrelated reasons: first, because the correlation between associational life and the generation of these values is often weaker than is often supposed, and second, because progress toward just and effective policy outcomes is usually associated with action across different sets of institutions – government and business as well as voluntary associations.

The achievement of the good society requires both norms of behavior that infuse institutions with values-based energy and direction, and political settlements that legitimize and sustain these values and directions in the polity. Working alone, voluntary associations can secure neither of these things, since norms and values are fostered in families, schools and workplaces as well as in associations, and political and legal ordering by government is required to secure all social contracts. In recent history, a rich associational life is correlated only weakly with the eradication of poverty and the achievement of other national development goals in "high performers" such as South Korea, Chile and Botswana, though, as chapter 1 pointed out, it has never been irrelevant. A strong, purposeful state and broad-based participation in the market economy have been as or more influential. Naturally, when development requires the overthrow and reconstruction of state institutions (as in Eastern Europe, the Arab Spring or South Africa), major social transformations do tend to be led by citizens and their associations, but, in general, nation-building, not civil society-building, is the core task of development in its early stages. Some societies (such as China) are making progress with a weak associational life, at least defined in Western terms, while others (such as the USA) have strong third sectors but continuing problems of inequality and discrimination. Americans gave more to charity in 2011 than ever before ($299 billion, to be exact), but America is no nearer to solving its pressing social problems.[10] Given these varying experiences, how is "a civil society" to be created?

Associational life and the good society

We saw in chapter 2 how structural and normative understandings of civil society became conflated through the experience of civic and political movements such as Solidarity in Poland and – on the other side of the Atlantic – through the arguments of neo-Tocquevillians, who saw voluntary associations as the "gene carriers" of the good society. If the good society is defined as one where free associations flourish, then the tendency to conflate these understandings is even stronger. The "demand for a return to civil society," as Daniel Bell has written, "is the demand for a return to a manageable scale of social life . . . which emphasizes voluntary associations . . . arguing that decisions should be made locally and should not be controlled by the state and its bureaucracies."[11] However, there are good reasons to doubt the link between ends and means that is implied in this statement, since, in Michael Walzer's oft-quoted words, "the associational life of civil society is the ground where all visions of the good are worked out and tested, *and* proved to be partial, incomplete and ultimately unsatisfying . . . there is no possibility of choosing, like the old anarchists, civil society alone."[12] Why not?

In Norman Rockwell's famous painting *Freedom of Speech*, the humble citizen stands tall, shining with integrity, to speak his mind at the local town-hall meeting. In the Rockwell school of civil society thinking, communities, citizens and associations are nearly always upright, honest and noble, but in the real world they are nearly always mixed in their motivations and their interests. This constitutes a difficult problem for the "civil society revivalists," as they have been called, since those in this school of thought insist that voluntary social interaction produces high and generalized levels of trust and cooperation, which in turn are essential for democracy and social progress.[13] Their key hypothesis is that communities, networks and associations are "micro-climates" in which skills are learned, values and loyalties consolidated, and caring and cooperation – instead of competition and violence – become the rational ways to behave, and there are three reasons why this should be true. First, the level and frequency of face-to-face interaction that are possible in associations or small communities mean that incentives for trusting and cooperative behavior are likely to be stronger: as a member of a small group, I can see or judge the consequences of my uncooperative actions and reap the rewards of cooperation from each of my colleagues – "you scratch my back and I'll scratch yours, or we both scratch out each other's eyes." Second, social norms are likely to be reinforced through familiarity and peer pressure, since either I agree to play by the rules or I join someone else's club. Third, the members of a group can see on a small scale that the welfare of the whole depends on the individual actions of its members, thereby anchoring the kinds of behavior that are essential if democracy is to function in the public interest at higher levels too.

The next step in the "revivalist" argument is to demonstrate that these generalized norms feed through into the effective operation of democracy, and from there to the good society since a functioning democracy should eventually produce a public consensus on good society goals. Nancy Rosenblum lists the "key virtues for democracy" as follows: "civility, or treating people identically and with easy spontaneity, and fairness, or speaking out against arbitrary injustice."[14] Whether membership in voluntary associations actually generates these virtues is debatable, but a link could certainly be made in theory, since regular interaction with groups of overlapping memberships should strengthen "civility" while incentives to cooperation should strengthen "fairness."

So far so good, until the genie of difference is introduced into the equation. Early in the work that eventually led to *Bowling Alone*, Robert Putnam's blockbuster about the "collapse and revival of American community," a seminar was held at the Harvard Divinity School to discuss the subject of social capital. Putnam, as expected, extolled the virtues of choirs, choral societies and other voluntary associations, until one member of the audience piped up with the following question: "But Bob, what is the choir *singing?*"[15] As this question implies, associational life per se is unlikely to guarantee a particular set of social norms and values whenever associations and their members vary widely in their characteristics, purposes and beliefs. "The rebirth of civil society is always riddled with dangers since it gives freedom to despots and democrats alike."[16]

The reality is that norms vary between different associations in the same society or culture and between different cultures and societies – not exactly rocket science, but crucial to a clear view of potential pathways to social progress. Notions of reciprocity, for example, are not the same in white America, African-American communities in the USA, tribal societies in Africa, Muslim or Jewish religious communities, and villages in China. Some norms – such as trust and even cooperation – have a different value for people in different situations. Neither can be considered unalloyed "goods," since one person's confidence may be abused by less scrupulous others, especially in societies shot through by inequality, corruption and exploitation – think of landlords in rural India, for example, governments who lie to their citizens, or the directors of the banks and insurance companies who were indicted after the global financial crash of 2008. Generally, poor people do best when they are "cautious reciprocators," that is, predisposed to cooperate but unafraid to retaliate when others take advantage of them. To be uncritically trusting when power is unequally distributed and information is imperfect is a dangerous strategy for advancement, so it is misleading to aggregate these norms at the level of communities, associations or societies as a whole. Both trust and mistrust must be discriminating.

Even if the same norms were universally interpreted to mean the same thing and weighted with the same importance, they might be put to different uses at the next level of specificity in defining the good society's ends and means. For example, people might develop high levels of trust for each other but lose it in the institutions – for example, government and the market – that are vital for promoting social goals. So voting may decline even as volunteering increases (exactly the correlation that has been observed for contemporary America, where associational life is in danger of becoming a substitute for politics).[17] Cooperation may be expressed in actions that are socially inclusive or exclusive, for or against affirmative action, tolerant of economic inequality or not. Different norms might even cancel each other

out, such as volunteering for the Ku Klux Klan, which does nothing for fairness but might still strengthen cooperation, at least with other members. The "greatest" or "long civic generation" that is praised by the revivalists for its vitality after the Second World War was also the generation in which the lynching of African-Americans reached its peak, Japanese-Americans were interned while their property was sold for a pittance, and racial discrimination in jobs, industry, education and voting became routine.[18] In any case, the principal ingredient in volunteering is enthusiasm, not necessarily an activism driven by a particular social vision. Voluntary associations are arenas for personal ambition and power as well as for sacrifice and service. "Pillar of the community, soccer coach, wife beater," as a sign on the New York subway reads. As in the case of the choir, the good society depends on what volunteers do and why they do it, not simply who they are.

Most important of all, norms and values do vary considerably between associations. At some point in civil society discussion, one bright spark will come up with the obvious question about the Mafia. "Is the Mafia a member?" they will ask, expecting the whole of civil society theory to come crashing down like a house of cards when they hear the answer "no." Since September 11, 2001, the disproving example of choice has been al-Qaeda, and no doubt another is waiting in the wings. But extreme examples like this can be dismissed as violent criminals, just as similar elements would be dismissed if they were criminals in government or criminals in business. Other cases are more significant, for example Lebanon (during that country's long civil war) and Rwanda (prior to the genocide in 1994), where strong networks of voluntary associations did foment inter-group violence. Rwanda had the highest density of associations in sub-Saharan Africa, while the "vast majority" of associations in Lebanon during the 1970s and 1980s were "exclusionary, divisive" and constantly at war with each other.[19] In both cases, associations were organized along ethnic or religious lines and mobilized politically, which at least in some eyes disqualifies them from civil society membership. In translation, Interahamwe, the name given to the Hutu killing-machine in Rwanda, means "those who attack together," a chilling echo of the claim that Timothy McVeigh and his fellow Oklahoma City bombers may have been members of bowling leagues in the USA, and that the students responsible for the Columbine High School massacre a year later reputedly spent their morning bowling with their classmates.[20] *Pace* Putnam, if killing, as among the Interahamwe, is a "civic duty," then better "bowling alone than conspiring together."[21] Clearly, the problem here is not collective action per se, but collective action allied to other factors that turn it in particular directions for good or for ill. But if this is the case, then the argument must hold for both the positive cases and the negative – meaning that generalized notions of associational life and its effects are unlikely to be tenable.

In any case, the most significant problems for civil society revivalists emerge not from the extreme clashes of values that characterize the behavior of terrorists such as McVeigh and bin Laden or the killers of civilians in zones of civil war, but from the ambiguous moral effects of ordinary, non-violent associations with different purposes and views – the inevitable result, of course, of the pluralism that civil society is supposed to protect. After all, civil society is known as the realm of "particularity" – the place where, whoever we are, we can find a home without asking for permission from above. This is why attempts to define away the problem of "uncivil" society inevitably founder in the gray waters of associational life, especially when allied to the whiff of authoritarian moralizing that often accompanies judgments about "who is in and who is out," and a tendency to romanticize the past in order to justify a return to ideologically driven "realities" in the present. Some associations could be excluded because they deliberately seek to destroy the rights of others to participate in civil society through violence, but judgments about the rest would be unlikely to meet a universal consensus. And although there is some evidence that positive norms and values feed through into high levels of performance among associations providing services to the poor or advocating on their behalf, there is no evidence that this is generally true in comparison to institutions doing similar things in the public and private sectors. Rather, the factors underlying outstanding performance seem to cut across these different institutions – high levels of accountability, for example, a clear focus, good listening skills, and the minimum degree of hierarchy that is needed to make good decisions. This is especially true for the supposed superiority of faith-based associations in America, which is not a surprising conclusion to anyone who has experienced incompetence from charities as well as from businesses or governments, but it may be discomfiting to those who wish to privilege one sector over others on grounds of ideology.

Given these high levels of difference and diversity, it is not surprising that the moral reality of associational life doesn't necessarily add up at the macro-level. Conditions in the Weimar Republic during the rise of Adolf Hitler are often cited to support this point – a dense network of citizens' groups unable or unwilling to counter the increasing power of the Nazi Party. Similar claims have been made about Italy under fascism (where the choirs that Putnam claims sustained Italian democracy sang Mussolini's tunes) and civil society in the Balkans after the death of Marshal Tito.[22] However, one doesn't have to look back in time for useful illustrations, since associational life in the aggregate is never uniform in its effects. Religious organizations are especially interesting in this respect, since they are home to both liberal and conservative elements, inclusionary and exclusionary norms of behavior, openness and prejudice. In the late 1980s, an unholy alliance between the Bulgarian orthodox church and chauvinist elements in politics fought to preserve "new forms of backwardness" as the country opened to the West (mirroring the emergence of Hindu nationalism in India), while right-wing populism in America has had gay and reproductive rights in its sights for a generation or more.[23] Are these examples of uncivil society, or merely illustrations of associations with different views on the "restless battlefield

of interests"?[24] The existence of diversity inevitably compli-
cates the link between forms and norms that lies at the heart
of neo-Tocquevillian thinking. Adam Seligman captures this
dilemma well: "when associations are ethically construed as
different normative universes, they represent not the realiza-
tion but the destruction of civil life . . . on the other hand,
when they are built around the principle of interest they
cannot mediate or mitigate interest-motivated action in the
name of some higher ethical unity."[25]

Inequality and discrimination pose particular problems for
civil society theory since they invest associations and their
members with different levels of resources that can be used
for individual advancement and not just the common interest. The biases introduced by education and income are especially pronounced in civic and political activity (the richer
and more educated you are, the more likely you are to vote,
make campaign contributions and participate in most classes
of associations, at least in America). So "although the decline
of civic engagement is contentious, the inequality of civic
engagement is unambiguous," a conclusion that was recon-
firmed by the same authors in 2012 almost twenty years after
their original surveys were carried out.[26] Large differentials
in the power of associations to make their voices heard,
advance their agendas and consolidate their own interpretation of shared norms in the public sphere are the enemy of
the good society, and of democracy. That is why reducing
inequality is a crucial part of any solution to the civil society
puzzle. Even more destructive is discrimination based on
race, caste, gender or sexual orientation, which is why some
NGOs in India use the concept of "twice-born civil society"
to underline the importance of eradicating such divisions
before society can be civil. The idea of civil society has also
been subjected to rigorous questioning from feminist critiques in an attempt to reveal its hidden biases and develop
more egalitarian theories for the future. Women are major
civic actors in and of themselves, of course, but gender con-
siderations have not been high on the priority list for most
civil society researchers. In reality, the composition of civil

society associations, the norms and practices they embody, the barriers that inhibit civic participation for some over others, and the operations and achievements of citizen groups and their leaders are all highly gendered.[27] We saw in chapter 2 how civic participation has declined among women in particular in the United States since the late 1950s. The fact that associational life is home to sexism, racism, homophobia and small-scale violence is distressing to civil society revivalists, but it must be faced if we are to identify the steps that can be taken to render associational life an effective vehicle for realizing social goals.

Recognition of these inequalities provides a clue to the final reason why associational life is always incomplete as a path to the good society. By themselves, voluntary associations cannot aggregate their interests in order to secure the political settlements that are crucial to development above the local level. This is especially true when strong but divided associations push against a weak state – as in the special-interest politics of the USA, interreligious conflicts in the Lebanese civil war, or the "anti-globalization" protests of Seattle and beyond (since no global government exists). Empirically this is not completely true, since shared interpretations of norms may develop among associations even if they are put to different uses, and high levels of self-organization and democratic representation can develop among like-minded sections of civil society, at least at certain times – when the interests of all associations in a country are threatened by a government, for example, or when associations come together to present a united front during times of democratic transition (the Philippines under Ferdinand Marcos comes to mind as one example). In general, however, associational life has to be politically ordered if the huge diversity of positions and interests is to be consolidated in service to some broader national or international agenda.

These observations do not mean that there are no connections between associational life, the cultivation of positive social norms and the aims of the good society, and in chapter

5 we will look at these connections in some detail. At their best, NGOs and other civic groups are characterized by attitudes of service and solidarity, beyond the particularities of any special interests. But such connections are always ambiguous. To say that a civil society "requires" trust and mutuality is true, but associational life doesn't generate these things by itself, especially in deeply fractured societies. Visions of the good society that rest on voluntary action alone will always be built on shifting sands.

States, markets and societies that are civil

If a strong civil society cannot create a society that is strong and civil, then what can? The answer lies through action *across* different institutions that is motivated by particular social values and directed at specific social goals, what Fowler and Biekart call "civic-driven change."[28] While governments, firms and families are not part of associational life as defined in chapter 2, they must be part of building the good society because they influence both social norms and achievements, and the political settlements that translate them into public policy. So instead of fixating on one sector to the exclusion of the others (whether market, state or civic), we should look for institutional arrangements that can secure the goals that have been arrived at in the public sphere. In the good society success is usually collective, especially at a time of "civil corporations," "uncivil society" and "network states."[29]

This process has to start by recognizing – as did Gramsci – that the family is central to shaping the values and dispositions of individuals. It may be somewhat romantic to claim, as does Stephen Carter, that "the family is a place where we die to the Self," but it is surely correct to say, at the deepest level, that families are or should be the first "civil societies," marked out by sacrifice and caring for the other.[30] Trust, cooperation and other more specific political attitudes all begin to be formed in family relationships. Family life (along with schooling and work) takes up far more of most people's

time than participation in associations, so it can be expected
to influence people's commitments especially strongly.

Unlike trust, love and compassion are more likely to be
less ambiguously positive in their effects, not because they
resolve higher-order social and political questions but because
they create a foundation for radically different modes of
behavior on which new solutions can be built. Defined by
the wonderfully named Institute for Research on Unlimited
Love at Case Western University, "the essence of love is to
affectively affirm as well as unselfishly delight in the well-
being of others, and to engage in acts of care and service on
their behalf, without exception, in an enduring and constant
way."[31] Not a bad foundation for the good society, it seems
to me, so the formation and nurturing of loving and supportive family relationships – in which both employers and
governments obviously play a role – is crucial to building a
society that is civil.

Civil society and the market

Beyond the role of businesses in helping to provide adequate
support structures like these by raising wages, benefits and
labor standards and encouraging their employees to be active
in civic life, it would have been odd, until fairly recently, to
emphasize the value of closer links between civil society and
the market. As we saw in chapter 1, some theorists do see
civil society as inseparable from the market economy, but
even enthusiasts like Gellner did not foresee a merger
between the two. That position has been altered dramatically
since the early 2000s by the arrival of hybrid institutions like
social enterprise and venture philanthropy, which are underpinned by the belief that business thinking and the logic of
the market should also be applied to civil society thinking.[32]
Supporters of this movement believe that the boundaries
between civil society and the market are collapsing. This is a
welcome development, they argue, because scarce resources
can then be allocated to civil society organizations that

produce the highest social returns in the most cost-effective ways. Civil society groups and businesses could even operate under a single set of principles that combine both social and financial criteria. However, the costs and benefits of these ideas are hotly contested.

Arguing in their favor are a raft of leaders from business and management consultancy like Julie Meyer, the CEO of Ariadne Capital in London: "the business of doing good should be just that," she says, "a business . . . it should not be left to governments, volunteers and non-profits."[33] There is palpable excitement about the possibilities of privatizing and commercializing the sphere of social action. In many ways this is the logical end point of the neo-liberal revolution that began in the early 1980s and that has since spread into healthcare, education, government and now civil society, as non-profit groups are drawn further and further into the structures of capitalism rather than acting as a counterweight. In the process, the last refuge of non-market values has been converted into one of the hottest properties of market-based investors.

The justification for this shift is that it is possible to improve both the financial sustainability and the social impact of civil society groups simultaneously by invoking market mechanisms, and in some areas of civic life this may be true. Take a group that is providing social services to an under-served population such as children with disabilities where public provision is weak, or an NGO that wants to get less labor-intensive cooking stoves to villages in Africa. Without the ability of markets to get these things to scale cheaply and efficiently, there would be little hope of achieving social goals in a way that allows the process to expand over time by generating profits, even if those profits are re-invested in the core mission of the group rather than distributed to shareholders (as in a conventional business). Developing successful social enterprises in this way does demand responsiveness to the disciplines of the market and the criteria and timeframes that are imposed by market-based investors.

Because these investors have detailed requirements for data on costs and returns, this movement is quite technocratic and control-oriented, ostensibly as a way of ensuring good results. Few of these investors seem interested in promoting independent, collective action at the grassroots level, though some of them do invest in advocacy causes that are both progressive and conservative. Generally, however, politics, power relations and social differences are things to be ignored or circumvented as barriers to success. As this quotation from the head of the Skoll Center for Social Entrepreneurship in Oxford makes clear, the older traditions of civil society action are seen as second-rate or no longer necessary, dismissed as hopelessly out of touch with today's new realities: "in the 21st Century, the march isn't the vehicle . . . social entrepreneurs are the new revolutionaries but they are not the placard-carrying types."[34] What civil society really needs is more business-style efficiency and discipline.

It isn't difficult to see what is questionable about these assumptions, however well-intentioned. At a philosophical level, identifying civil society with the market constitutes the kind of "category error" that occurs when values, principles and mechanisms that work in one context are assumed to generate the same results in another. But competition and cooperation are very different things, as are "exit, voice and loyalty," as Hirschman pointed out.[35] "Exit" – the freedom of consumers to switch to a different supplier at any given time – is crucial to the ability of markets to channel resources to their most efficient use, but this would be disastrous for communities and civil society groups who rely on voice and loyalty from their members or constituents. The roles of civil society and the market may overlap where gaps must be filled in the provision of socially useful services and goods, but civil society's core functions have always been social, cultural and political, not economic. New institutions like social enterprises are vital to the emergence of a healthier "social economy" and they should be encouraged, but they cannot produce a stronger civil society however successful they may be, since that is a task of a qualitatively different kind.

Social goods are "incommensurable," meaning that they have no common measure of value, unlike profits, prices and financial returns in economics. Therefore, decisions about which groups we join, support or volunteer for in civil society are based on different views of what is valuable, rooted in personal preferences and beliefs.[36] What some would factor into the equation as a cost would be measured as a benefit by others. Take, for example, the amount of time devoted by civil society groups to the messy processes of democratic decision-making and debate. In 2013 the Girl Scouts of America were riven with dissent over just this question when the central office decided to merge many local chapters in order to save on costs, a move which also risks losing the civic energy and democratic involvement that come from decentralized activity.[37] Unlike firms, most civic groups are not "substitutable" for each other because affiliations are based on affinity, not on the price and quality of the goods or services provided. And the "social" in "social enterprise" usually refers to a target group in society rather than to the social structures, power relations and collective action strategies that mark out civil society activities.

Social economy enthusiasts would say that blending civil society and the market produces a new and tasty cocktail, but the evidence suggests that mixing oil and water may be the more appropriate analogy since so many trade-offs are involved. They include "mission drift" when groups are pulled in radically different directions, and the adoption of technocratic modes of operation that constrain what civic groups can do.[38] They may develop "perfect eyesight" in the form of sophisticated management information and the like, but lose their social and political vision in the process. As more and more non-profits are encouraged to "behave more like a business" – calculating returns on their investment, designing complex metrics, presenting themselves as competing charity brands and internalizing other aspects of market values and behavior – their effectiveness as civil society actors may actually decrease because their role in building "small-d" democracy will be displaced.

There may also be a trend toward monopoly or oligopoly (as in financial markets) if resources are attracted to organizations that can out-compete, or simply out-muscle and out-advertise, their counterparts. There is already a belief among market-oriented philanthropists that there are "too many" non-profits and that more mergers should be encouraged. Market-based approaches may also dilute the "gift relationships" that are the essence of civic life – the reciprocity and voluntary, "other-directed" behavior that differ radically from transactional relationships. Overall, "an emphasis on entrepreneurialism and the satisfaction of individual self-interest is incompatible with democratic accountability, citizenship and an emphasis on collective action for the public interest."[39] Civil society needs more "main street" involvement, not more "Wall Street" influence and direction.

However, these gloomy consequences can be avoided. The first step in doing so is to acknowledge that social enterprise and other similar experiments are an important part of the conversation about the rise of the social economy, but a small part of the debate about civil society and its future. When used sparingly and in ways that are discriminating, these new approaches can be very helpful in identifying additional routes to financial sustainability for civil society groups that have something to trade or sell in the marketplace, but they must be used only when they are appropriate and where negative trade-offs can be managed. Thinking back to the ecosystems of collective action that were described in chapter 2, one would expect that different kinds of groups and activities would require different forms of financing and support. Hence traditional civil society groups and newer hybrids are not necessarily in competition with each other, just as screwdrivers and hammers complement each other in a toolkit – unless, of course "you only have a hammer," as the saying goes, in which case "everything becomes a nail." There is something of that prophecy contained in the current hype surrounding social enterprises, venture philanthropy and the like.

The second step forward is to find more ways of increasing the civic and political impact of experiments in the social economy. For example, community banks, credit unions and other collective ownership arrangements show how the economic surplus can be shared and re-invested under democratic control instead of being appropriated and hoarded by private financial institutions. Community-controlled economic development initiatives can channel some of their profits into locally governed agencies and programs. New forms of money and exchange (like alternative and non-cash currencies, and no-interest financing) are already being used to revitalize communities in settings like Brazil, where the Green Life Bank accepts wheelbarrows of recyclable garbage in exchange for notes that can be spent in local stores.[40] A non-profit called stone circles offers "radical hospitality" packages at discounted rates for other NGOs at its rural retreat center in North Carolina, and channels the funds into its community organizing programs. Make the Road New York works with the Brooklyn Co-Operative Credit Union to help its members obtain loans to cover their membership dues if they experience temporary economic hardship. Not many social enterprises or non-profits are thinking as creatively as this, but groups like stone circles and Make the Road are demonstrating that market mechanisms can be used without eroding activism and solidarity. As one element of a broader strategy they can yield real benefits without destroying the collective underpinnings of civil society action.

Civil society and the state

Experiments like these show some micro-level promise, but they are unlikely to combat macro-level inequalities of power, or address the hidden hierarchies of gender, race, sexuality and class that often underpin them. Dealing explicitly with these inequalities is a precondition for societies that are civil, and this task must include government action to "level the playing field" by legislating against discrimination, protecting labor and other standards, guaranteeing adequate social security and childcare arrangements, and doing all the other things that civil society associations, firms and families can't or won't do by themselves. America's unwillingness to accept this fact drives its desire to seek solutions to structural problems through voluntary action, a journey that is destined to end in tears.

For example, women may gain more access to employment through the marketplace or non-profit support programs, but they still need legislation on equal pay and childcare provision in order to take advantage of these opportunities. The disconnection that poor people typically feel is as much from the structures of economic and political power as from each other, so a strong, democratically accountable state is just as important as associational life to the eradication of poverty. Even Alexis de Tocqueville acknowledged that "if men are to remain civilized or to become so, the art of associating together must grow and improve in the same ratio in which the equality of conditions is increased." "Good neighbors cannot replace good government."[41]

This is a difficult message to communicate, however, to some neo-Tocquevillians, who still see government as a bugbear despite the role of the state in securing the preconditions for equal civic participation and legal protection for associations. For them, it is moral values that have collapsed since 1945, not the support structures that enable moral beings to act as citizens, carers, parents and volunteers, as well as workers and consumers. There is a clear fault-line between those who see associational life as irredeemably particular (requiring government intervention to enforce universal norms, rights and standards) and those who see a negotiated consensus in civil society as the only social contract that will last. This split is paralleled by a similar divide between those who claim that social mores are structured by politics, and those who claim that politics are structured by social mores. Seeing "government as the domain of common purpose and identity" and civil society as the realm of "anarchy, private oppression, and the private engrossment of collective resources" may seem fanciful at a time when private interests seem to have more influence over government than ever before, but, since states retain a monopoly over the means of violence and coercion, it is difficult to see how any other set of institutions can act as guarantors of equal treatment in this way.[42] Zygmunt Bauman argues that "zones of civility" in everyday life are *only* possible if the means of institutional violence are stored elsewhere. In this sense it would be disastrous if we were to "give up on the state's ability to establish the rule of law or democracy through elections and legislatures, and instead give civic associations – the political equivalent of the private sector – a chance to do their thing."[43]

In any case, major social transformations or systemic changes in politics and economics have rarely been achieved by associations acting alone, even when channeled through broad-based social movements. Achieving these things requires a series of reforms across society so that states, markets and intermediary associations harness their different energies to some common purpose – as countries in East Asia did from the 1950s to the 1980s, or as successful states such as Kerala and West Bengal have done in India. In Kerala, this took the form of agreements between a democratic government and a powerful labor movement that resulted in social and economic gains far more impressive than in other Indian states (though this record is now being questioned by high rates of out-migration and a fall-off in industrial investment and innovation).[44] In Taiwan and South Korea, a less democratic state and a weaker set of intermediary associations still developed sufficient synergy to transform the structure of production at rates unknown in history, though of course there were many other factors in play that had little to do with state–society relations. These episodes of constructive engagement have all been based on social contracts between governments, business and civil society that secure a minimum level of consensus around the trade-offs that characterize the process of development – between growth and redistribution; short-term sacrifices and long-term benefits; private, public and collective interests. What is the key to successful development? "It's the polity, stupid" – not "generalized trust" but social, economic and political energy strategically directed at the specifics of each set of challenges through coordinated action across different sets of institutions. That is the path to the good society.

One conclusion is clear: those who search for the good society must find their allies – and identify their enemies – wherever they can, among those elements of government, business and associational life that share a similar agenda, since not all do. However, if the good society requires coordinated action between different institutions all pulling in the same direction, how do societies decide the direction in which they want to go, and whether it is the right one as circumstances change? How do societies make collective choices, negotiate trade-offs, and reconcile ends with means in ways that are just and effective? For answers to these questions we must turn to the theory of the public sphere.

4
Civil Society as the Public Sphere

In nineteenth-century Bengal, a long-forgotten but once celebrated exchange took place between Rabindranath Tagore and Nabinchandra Sen.[1] The subject of debate between the famous poet and his equally erudite opponent was the appropriateness of public mourning, a concept very different to the private grief of traditional Hindu teaching and – according to Sen – very much an invention of India's colonial masters, the British. Tagore's position revolved around the development of a new and necessary responsibility to mourn the deaths of those who had devoted their lives to the struggle for independence in full public view, as part of a strategy to consolidate new norms and alliances across old and familiar boundaries. Without such a public sensibility, progress would be much more difficult to achieve because pre-existing divisions and the primacy of different lives lived in private would make it impossible to solidify a united front in favor of reform. "Publics are formed when we turn from our separate affairs to face common problems, and face each other in dialogue and discussion."[2]

The concept of a "public" – a whole polity that cares about the common good and has the capacity to deliberate about it democratically – is central to civil society thinking. The development of shared interests, a willingness to cede some territory to others, the ability to see something of oneself in those who are different and work together more effectively as a result – all these are crucial attributes for effective governance, practical problem-solving and the peaceful resolution of our differences. In its role as the "public sphere," civil society becomes the arena for argument and deliberation as well as for association and institutional collaboration: a "non-legislative, extra-judicial, public space in which societal differences, social problems, public policy, government action and matters of community and cultural identity are developed and debated."[3] The extent to which such spaces thrive is crucial to the health of a democracy, since if only certain truths are represented, if alternative viewpoints are silenced by exclusion or suppression, and if one set of voices is heard more loudly than those of others (those of the wealthy, for example, or of a particular ideological orientation), then no genuine sense of the "public" interest can be negotiated. A good example would be the debate over genetically modified foods, an issue that arouses strong views on all sides and whose outcome will be crucial to the health and welfare of millions of people as consumers and producers all across the world. In these circumstances, an objective reading of the options and the evidence is a prerequisite for coming to some legitimate resolution, but this is precisely what is lacking from the current mix of corporate lobbying, sensational media coverage and blanket condemnation by protestors. Such debates are the very stuff of a democracy.

Ideas about the public sphere stretch back at least to Aristotle, for whom a disposition to seek each other's company and form "political friendships" in search of the common good was characteristic of all good citizens. Since only certain people qualified as citizens in ancient Greece this was not a particularly "public" public, and later theories of the public sphere addressed this problem by stressing the power relations that permeate communications and the virtues of inclusive conversation. John Keane traces the history of ideas about the public sphere in three different phases: as a weapon against despots in eighteenth-century Europe and North America; as a means, throughout the twentieth century, to critique the increasing commodification of areas of life thought to be free from the influence of the market; and today, as a defense of public communications in service to democracy.[4]

We saw in chapter 1 how a strong tradition of thinking in Keane's first and second phases grew up in the USA, where it was rooted in the Founding Fathers' belief in a system of government in which opinions would be refined through public debate and practical compromise. This system was undermined from the very beginning by inequalities of voice and vote based on discrimination, and by the gradual commercialization of the means of communication through which publics formed and engaged with each other beyond the traditional face-to-face interactions that characterized small, homogeneous communities. It was these concerns that led later writers in America – such as John Dewey, Hannah Arendt and Richard Sennett – to lament the decline of the public sphere as a result of increasing self-absorption and the commercial colonization of the media, a writing tradition that continues in the USA today through the work of Harry Boyte, Sara Evans and others such as the Kettering Foundation who see civil society as an autonomous space for generating democratic ideas and innovations.

By common consent, however, the most successful attempt to elaborate these ideas came from Jürgen Habermas, who theorized in highly elaborate terms the existence of a "discursive public sphere" that enabled citizens to talk about common concerns in conditions of freedom, equality and non-violent interaction. These qualifying conditions are crucial, because they establish a boundary within which conversations must take place if they are to qualify as democratic, and therefore effective in generating the outcomes the public sphere is supposed to produce. In Habermas's thinking, participants in public conversations will come to a consensus about the great issues of the day through the force of rational argument. It is the best ideas that will triumph, not the loudest voice – a somewhat quaint conclusion given the inequalities that characterize all contemporary societies. Theorists who follow Habermas lay great stress on the ethics and structures of these discourses, since unless they are carefully ordered there is no possibility that the public sphere can work as theory predicts. Habermas's ideas have also been criticized as ethnocentric, based as they are on a particular reading of rationality that is rooted in the linear thinking of the Enlightenment. Nevertheless, the conviction that groups of people can change their minds by engaging with each other non-violently is critical to democracy, both because it makes political consensus possible and because it tends to mitigate extremist views on all sides of the political spectrum. Like rocks in a stream, the sharpness of different perspectives can be softened over time as they knock against one another.

A public sphere, says Keane, "is a particular type of spatial relationship between two or more people . . . connected by means of communication . . . in which non-violent controversies erupt . . . concerning the power relations operating within their given milieu of interaction."[5] Early examples included the coffee houses of eighteenth-century London and Edinburgh, the fabled town-hall meetings of revolutionary New England, and the debates that animated the public squares of all historic cities. Contemporary examples range from the "micro" public spheres of literary circles and book clubs, citizens' juries and "deliberation days," through public radio and television, independent newspapers, facilitated debates, referenda and deliberative opinion polls at the national level, to potentially global public spheres such as the World Social Forum or public-access Internet sites such as that of openDemocracy, which bills itself as an arena for intelligent conversation in cyberspace between people of different and dissenting views.[6] All societies possess a range of these public spheres at different levels, which rise and fall according to the issues at hand and the circumstances of the moment. A single, unified public sphere would be impossible at any significant scale.

Theories of the public sphere provide a powerful framework for interpreting the role played by civil society in social change, though their implications are often ignored by the neo-Tocquevillians or reduced by donor agencies to preserving the institutions of the independent media and building the communications capacities of NGOs. A functioning public sphere does rest on elements of the first two definitions of civil society explored in chapters 2 and 3, but it is more than the sum of these parts because it is the vehicle through which associational life and the good society connect to each other over time. As Leonardo Avritzer has shown for Latin America, participatory publics that are animated by free and autonomous voluntary associations provide a better way to guard against anti-democratic forces than the democratic elitism that was practiced across the continent in earlier times.[7] Inclusive and objective public deliberation is feasible only through channels that are not completely captured by states or markets, so the condition of associational life and the regulatory frameworks imposed by government are always important factors. On the other hand, what takes place in the public sphere is, or is assumed to be, marked out by the normative values of the good society – for example, tolerance for dissent; a willingness to argue without quitting the debate when other, more persuasive, voices take the stage; and a commitment to "truth telling" in the traditions of the US civil rights movement. These norms are crucial if problems are genuinely to be resolved in the public interest, since there is no other way the public interest can be defined. The public sphere is explicitly concerned with fashioning a democratic framework for the development and expression of collective visions about the basic "rules of the game" – the judgments, priorities and trade-offs that guide the evolution of all societies.

Theories of the public sphere demand a return to the practice of politics, not as an elite occupation in which some of the public take part once every four or five years through elections, but as an ongoing process through which "active citizens" can help to shape both the ends and the means of the good society. Consciously or not, these ideas form the basis for the current and widespread revival of interest in "civic agency"; direct, deliberative and participatory democracy; and "dialogic politics" as an essential complement to the representative components of political systems in contexts as diverse as Scottish devolution, village India, neighborhood councils in Los Angeles, participatory budgeting in Brazil, and the poverty reduction strategy papers promulgated by the World Bank across the developing world.[8] Harry Boyte, one of the leading figures in the American civic agency movement, has written powerfully about the need to "de-professionalize politics and re-connect citizens to public life" through movements such as Minnesota Works Together, a state-wide effort to strengthen civic activity in neighborhoods, change the culture of higher education so that colleges and universities become vehicles for civil society engagement, and introduce new forms of cross-party political action among elected representatives.[9] Both participation and deliberation are necessary, though sometimes they conflict with each other because conversations are so difficult whenever attitudes are entrenched.[10] Nevertheless, the key element in all these initiatives is direct participation by large numbers of ordinary people in shaping the decisions that affect their lives and creating new publics in the process. In this sense, civil society – as a set of capacities – and politics – as a set of processes – become united in the public sphere, providing an essential antidote to the depoliticization and fatalism that are so marked in contemporary societies.

Why is the public sphere important?

Dialogic politics offers a route – and perhaps the only route – to reach a legitimate normative consensus around a plurality of interests and positions, assuming certain conditions are met – equality of voice and access, in particular, and a minimum of censorship so that the relevant information is available to all. Politics cannot be just unless the full range of views and interests is represented in a process in which all the protagonists agree to collaborate toward a resolution. At the very least, conversations in the public sphere can provide a reasoned justification for majority decisions, so helping to avoid the "tyranny" of a weakly elected government. This was something that had concerned much earlier theorists of democracy such as John Stuart Mill, who warned that the secret ballot would encourage voters to "choose the politicians who most pandered to their interests rather than voting for the public good."[11] The public sphere, by contrast, is centrally concerned with the processes of opinion- and will-formation that precede or surround the act of voting.

For Habermas, all modern states face a crisis of legitimacy that is rooted in the commodification of the public sphere, a process, he argues, that prevents publics from shaping state policy. Instead, they are increasingly manipulated *by* it. While the depth of this "crisis" can be contested, it is clear that major social change can only come about when sufficient public debate has sorted through the issues and a community emerges to support it. Amitai Etzioni uses the example of action against smoking, which arrived after thirty years of public discussion, to illustrate this point.[12] The emergence of corporate social responsibility, widespread public debate about the legitimacy of intervention in Iraq, Libya and Syria, and rising concerns about the costs of globalization are other examples of the same process at work today. The common interest can only be found through democratic struggle and debate – we cannot find it unless we look for it together. Solutions are more likely to hold when all social groups have a say in the answers and a stake in their outcomes. We may never share a common vision of ends and means in the good society, but we can all be committed to a process that allows everyone to share in defining how these different visions are reconciled.

In addition to consensus-making, public spheres play another role that is crucial to social progress: through the engagement of the maximum number of minds and eyes on any particular problem, solutions are more likely to be found.

Dialogic politics is continually engaged in a search for better ways forward, and since no one group holds a monopoly over wisdom (or even knowledge and information), these journeys must be democratic. As the political philosopher John Keane once told me, democracies are "long-term experiments in the capacity of citizens to live without secure foundations. We are all required to practice daily the art of living on the edge." Only politics, as Machiavelli famously taught, creates the possibility for maneuver and forward movement. The public sphere is important because it brings to the surface alternatives – new answers to old questions, challenges to the orthodox, and the occasional revolutionary surprise. In this sense, civil society signifies the "freedom to imagine something different," for, as Oscar Wilde once quipped, "a map of the world without Utopia marked on it is not a map worth having."[13] It is no accident that the World Social Forum picked "another world is possible" as its organizing slogan.

In the public sphere, all ideas and opinions are valid until proven otherwise. Totalitarianism, by contrast, replaces debate about the merits of an argument with an inquiry about the motives of the individuals involved – the tactic used by Stalin to silence intellectuals in Russia and by others in contemporary democracies to silence new manifestations of dissent. Margaret Thatcher's infamous double dicta – that "there is no alternative" and "there is no such thing as society" – are natural bedfellows, since in the absence of social networks and associations no "room" for argument exists. Theories of the public sphere also stress the diffusion of power that is essential to democratic debate and the exercise of accountability by citizens over government, business and their own associations. Accountability requires an active conversation between these institutions and the public (whether as clients, members, citizens or consumers), along with the high levels of transparency and the free flow of information that enable abuses to be exposed. Restrictions on the flow of information will damage the public sphere severely.

Most important of all, the public sphere helps different groups to find a balance between personal autonomy and the demands of the social whole, thus resolving the dilemma that has lain at the heart of civil society thinking since the days of the ancient Greeks. As previous chapters have shown, civil society is the land of difference, the place where we find meaning in our lives as people of different faiths, interests, perspectives and agendas. But the governance of complex societies and the preservation of peaceful coexistence require that some of these particularities are surrendered to the common interest, in the form of rules, laws, norms and other agreements that cut across the views of different communities, and to which all citizens subscribe. The application of these rules is ultimately the task of government and other institutions of the state, but civil society also plays a role in both legitimizing government intervention and imposing its own informal settlements through voluntary codes of conduct and other self-organizing principles. Without a functioning public sphere, neither would be possible, since no mechanisms would exist to negotiate the rules of the social game.

A successful civil society is one that supports the peaceful expression of these multiple identities without fracturing into a myriad of disconnected agendas – the place where we can celebrate our differences within a common commitment to the interests of a public. As an (admittedly parochial) example, take the case of the Church of the Holy Apostle in Manhattan, which every Friday meticulously clears away all Christian symbols before handing over to the local, but temporarily homeless, Jewish Congregation of Beth Simchatto-rah for the Sabbath. They in turn take equal care to return this space to its owners after their worship has been completed, providing, in microcosm, a vision of a public sphere in which different communities can practice their own rituals while sharing in the common resources provided by the building, carefully maintained by each for the other. These principles operate at higher levels too. Only by reaching out beyond our particularities – by voting for someone from a different group, appreciating the literatures and customs of different traditions and speaking, literally and metaphorically, many different languages – do we qualify as members of a wider whole. Otherwise, civil society remains the mere agglomeration of private interests. This is why philosophers from Hannah Arendt to Michael Walzer have seen moral maturity as a willingness to welcome diversity *and* seek the common good together among citizens whose interests, at least sometimes, reach further than themselves and their familiars.[14] Dispositions of this kind rest on the formation of democratic identities broad enough to respect differences when they are healthy and attack them when they are not, such as racism, sexism, homophobia and a failure to value the lives and life chances of others as dearly as one's own. And public spheres provide the venues for deliberating over which differences fall into each of these camps, going beyond a shallow interpretation of pluralism (defending our differences against each other) to forge a common yet inclusive framework of norms and values. In civil society, difference may be central or irrelevant, something to be celebrated or a cause of deep concern. The goal is to ensure that all decisions about the *meaning* of difference are democratic.[15] This is why inequality and discrimination are enemies of the public sphere, and why fundamentalism, especially when expressed in violence, is the most dangerous enemy of all. Fundamentalists of all persuasions refuse to accept that shared truths can be negotiated or that different versions of the truth can coexist – read blind obedience and absolute righteousness as the mirror image of dialogic politics. Such attitudes violate the basic rules of engagement of the public sphere as a place where "strangers can meet each other and not draw the knife."[16]

When communications are privatized, the possibilities of negotiated consensus decline, opening the way for conflicts between different versions of the truth sustained by their own exclusive structures of discussion, scholarship and journalism. Something of this sort happened in the Balkans after the death of Marshal Tito, when press reporters, radio and television covered the same stories from the perspectives of the different Yugoslav republics. When war began in Croatia and soon spread to Bosnia, Croats became *Ushtashe* to the Serbian media, Serbs became "Chetniks" to the Croats, and Muslims became "Islamic fundamentalists" to reporters everywhere.[17] As the structures of communication became fragmented along ethnic lines, mutual stereotypes played an important role in channeling ancient hatreds into large-scale violence. What disappeared (and are still absent from the region, despite foreign aid to media projects that stretch across these divisions) were forums directed at creating those sensibilities that occupied Rabindranath Tagore in nineteenth-century Bengal – public spheres to bind different groups together in common cause.

In addition, one of the legacies of the civil society revivalists has been a particular understanding of "civility" as politeness, not debate or disagreement. Ex-President George W. Bush, for example, aimed to "lower the political temperature" in Congressional debates over Iraq by conducting them "with all civility," but this is a distortion of what civility originally meant. Civility, from Aristotle to Stephen Carter, assumes that we will disagree, often profoundly, but calls on us to resolve our disagreements peacefully. Every other form of activity – from street protest to satire – is welcome in the public sphere. Active citizens need suspicious minds to probe and challenge, minds that are unafraid of speaking truth to power whenever that is needed. Avoiding debate is never the sign of a robust civic culture (political controversy is educative in and of itself), just as recoiling when challenged is not the quality of good citizens. Nina Eliasoph, a sociologist who has studied the conversations of volunteers in America, found that public debates about politics were frowned on as "divisive" or "uncivil," so that people's most important thoughts were relegated to their private interactions.[18] With attitudes like this it is not surprising that democracy is in trouble. The real exemplar of civility is not Miss Manners but Rosa Parks, someone who was brave enough to activate her citizenship in the public interest on a segregated bus in Montgomery, Alabama, even at the risk of being extremely "impolite."

America's love–hate relationship with identity politics does not help, leading to all sorts of contortions about what can be said about whom and how, without landing those concerned in court. Political correctness can, of course, be seen as a crucial defense against racism, sexism, homophobia and verbal violence, and as a positive affirmation of the value of diversity. But when taken to extremes (when difference cannot be named as the issue, or not the issue, on its own terms) it can have a deadening effect on the quality and depth of public engagement, resulting in a superficial consensus because people from different groups fear to "read each other's stories," still less understand and internalize their implications for a life lived in common. When arguments are curtailed too early, the public sphere can produce an illusion of agreement that disguises differences by class and income, race and gender, excluding the unorthodox and eliding ideological fractures in ways that are convenient for those in authority. People in power, whoever they are, can bear little of the truth as told to them by others or those within society who happen to be different.

Contemporary public spheres: threats and opportunities

It is clear from the argument thus far that public spheres form a crucial component of a thriving civil society. However, they are also vulnerable to many different threats. "The public domain is both priceless and precarious," writes David Marquand, requiring constant care and attention to prevent the active "enfeebling" that is promulgated by the market and the state.[19] In recent years, laments for the decline or erosion of the public sphere have grown more urgent, and the blame is usually laid at the doors of Rupert Murdoch and other media barons.[20] This is unsurprising, since such threats emerge most obviously from the increasing commercialization and concentrated ownership of the media and other vehicles for free expression, and from state control in authoritarian settings when combined with restrictions on more basic rights of information and association, especially in the aftermath of September 11, 2001, and the ensuing "war on terrorism."[21] Independent investigations of news coverage of the terrorist attacks on New York and Washington, DC, concluded that journalists on *Time* and *Newsweek* were unwittingly complicit in government communication strategies designed to rally public support, not to facilitate a public debate, a worrying illustration of the hollowing-out that has taken place over the last few years in the strength and quality of independent journalism in America.

Revelations in 2013 that phone and email records in the USA were subject to widespread surveillance by the National Security Agency raised numerous objections from those who feared the criminalization of investigative journalism under the guise of anti-terrorist operations, to go along with increasingly aggressive prosecutions of government whistleblowers and the chilling effects of investigations into charities by the Internal Revenue Service that were triggered by words such as "progressive," "advocacy," "Tea Party" and "Occupy."[22] This is not a recipe for a healthy public sphere, even if US government intervention is relatively soft when compared to the levels of outright violence and repression that regularly occur in countries such as Egypt, Uganda, China and Bahrain.

Other threats to the public sphere include the distortion of politics by money and moneyed interests; sound bites and slanging matches as a substitute for rigorous debate; overspecialized and elitist education systems that turn out idiots savants; a narrow interpretation of intellectual property rights that favors business over open access to ideas; and the effects of modern capitalism in reducing the time and energy most people can devote to active citizenship – it being difficult to "engage in the public sphere" after a twelve-hour or two-job day without any help with childcare. When the pressure is on, most of us succumb to the temptations of "couch potato" life in front of our television screens.

In fact all of the things that are required to animate the public sphere are under constant threat – energetic and knowledgeable citizens, independent networks and associations through which they can engage with each other, and the forums and arenas in which these engagements can take place. The result is that the public sphere cannot function effectively in resolving public-policy dilemmas – such as healthcare and social security, for example, in the USA, or an effective system for the peaceful resolution of disputes at the international level. Instead, these dilemmas remain embedded – sometimes frozen – in polities that cannot solve them. The underlying problem is a general one – the privatization or suppression of the "public" in every sphere of life and the pillaging of that which belongs to all of us in favor of private interests, whether it be unspoiled open spaces, clean air, genetic diversity, the Internet or the processes of politics themselves.[23]

In this context, it is not surprising that the communicative structures of the public sphere have met with a similar fate, with mergers between companies such as AOL Time Warner, Disney and Bertelsmann bringing different elements of the communications chain together under one authority. These developments may threaten the independence, diversity and diffusion of power that are essential if the public sphere is to operate as theory predicts. The unwillingness of many governments to regulate these mergers and monitor their implications makes this situation even worse, despite the fact that most physical structures of communication – for example, cable and telephone wires – run along public rights of way. It cannot be accidental that there has been so little coverage of campaign-finance reform measures that would halt political donations from broadcasters during successive US elections; or that portions of proposed legislation that would cost broadcasters millions of dollars in lost revenues are stripped after intense lobbying from the telecommunications industry; or that proposed global agreements on "trade-related intellectual property rights" have been so heavily pushed by such telecommunications and media lobby groups as the Motion Picture Association of America and the US-based International Intellectual Property Alliance, along with such corporations as Microsoft and AOL Time Warner. The

US Congress has already extended the terms of copyright eleven times since the early 1970s. In similar vein, Larry Lessig argues that the increasing commercialization and private ownership of the codes and architecture of the Internet by Google, Microsoft and others will destroy its potential as a source for innovation and support for new forms of "virtual" citizen action, an issue explored below.[24]

There are other problems that increasingly affect public and private media alike – including a general dumbing down of content, for example, the lure of celebrity rather than a commitment to explore the issues that affect the lives of ordinary citizens, and overly aggressive interviewing techniques that are a million miles away from the rational discourses envisaged by Jürgen Habermas. "Don't try to refute your opponents, just silence them through intimidation." These problems are all significant, but perhaps even more important are the pervasive inequalities that threaten the very foundation of the democratic public sphere. Whatever the theory concludes, the reality of dialogic politics is one of continued, entrenched inequality in voice and access and the domination of certain orthodoxies over others, which legitimizes ideas through raw power instead of through the power of rational argument between different but equal actors. This removes the central plank of Habermas's ideas, since it allows one group to impose a particular interpretation of the public interest on others. That fact that all public spheres are fractured by inequality is another reason why a single, unified public sphere or determination of the public interest is difficult to envisage, and perhaps may even be undemocratic in and of itself. Nevertheless, if social and economic realities do obstruct the workings of the public sphere, what actions can be taken to "level the playing field" so that public engagement at least has a chance to operate democratically?

Despite a tendency to do so in some quarters, one cannot ignore private interests or identities in order to make a public (that would be akin to baking a cake from the icing down). Such interests (which may be perfectly legitimate in and of themselves) have to be acknowledged and moved through systematically via engagement and debate. Nor can groups that have historically been isolated and marginalized be expected to enter the public sphere on equal terms – African-Americans in the USA, for example, Roma communities across Eastern Europe, or grassroots groups from Africa in the global public sphere. Strong bridges of public engagement rest on strong bonds of capacity and confidence within communities, especially those that have been subjugated in the past. "What matters to us," says the Citizen Organizing Foundation in the UK, "is not consensus, nor even harmony, but a stake in the ongoing dynamic of controversy, resolution and change."[25] Consensus, for all the reasons explored so far, does matter, but it has to be a real consensus and not simply an agreement between elites. One cannot long for a vibrant public sphere and avoid the political conflicts that drive people into or out of it. The best consent, let's remember, emerges from dissent, not from the rosy glow of polite conversation that fuels liberal fantasies about social transformation.

All this spells *contention*. "The supposed incivility of contemporary politics stems from the twin emergence of civically and politically engaged issue constituencies that have mobilized enough clout to no longer be ignored, and a continuing counter-mobilization among those who rue their rise from marginalization."[26] Accepting "incivility," if this is what it is, seems a paradoxical condition for civil society, but it is especially important because the ability to argue is likely to increase the influence of the materially less powerful even when progress in removing these inequalities is slow ("punching above one's weight," in UK Foreign Office terms). Providing more spaces – physical and virtual – in which public engagement is integrated is also vital. In the USA today, there are few places where different ethnic, religious and income groups regularly meet with each other, and many civic associations have failed to address key issues of diversity. This is not because people are less willing to engage, but because the opportunities to make connections outside one's own group in public have been diminished. Those who do take part in public discussions must also see some short-term benefits from their involvement, requiring reforms in the political system (such as curbing the power of lobbyists) so that there is a genuine chance of influencing politics through participation in the public sphere as well as voting.

New opportunities for strengthening public spheres

There is, however, another side to this gloomy story, and it is one that has generated more attention than almost anything else in the civil society debate in recent years. This is the "digital age," the use of information and communication technologies (or ICTs) to promote civic interaction via social media of different kinds. There is no doubt that these developments have changed the landscape of civil society action, or that they will continue to do so in the future, but the long-term implications of these changes have given rise to a passionate debate between enthusiasts and skeptics.

Certain things are not disputed: new technologies lower the costs and increase the speed, ease and reach of information-exchange and response, enabling a level of access to knowledge, opinions and ideas that has never before existed, so long as people have access to the Internet. Authors such as Clay Shirky, Manuel Castells and the Google chairman Eric Schmidt see this as a revolutionary advance that changes everyone and everything – from the ways in which we organize ourselves in civil society and politics, to new forms of work, play and education, to the evolution of a new sense of our own power and identity, and even a "Future Perfect" if Steven Johnson is to be believed.[27] These positions embrace a sense of both "cyber-utopianism" and "Internet-centrism" as described by their chief critic Evgeny Morozov.[28] The former focuses on the "inherent" democratizing effects of social media, and the latter emphasizes the underlying cultural shifts they are assumed to bring about, such as flatter forms of networked organizations with no need for hierarchy or centralized leadership or leaders, and the supposed superiority of "crowds" over "experts" when decisions need to be made and knowledge must be aggregated for action.

To support their sense of optimism, the cyber-enthusiasts cite a long list of examples from recent civil society activity, including the rising influence of global campaigning networks such as Avaaz and The Rules; domestic successes in mobilizing protests throughout the Arab Spring, the "color revolutions" in Georgia, Ukraine and elsewhere, and the rapid appearance and spread of Occupy encampments and the "indignados" movement in Spain during 2012; advances in democracy (especially political accountability) through the use of cell-phones for election-monitoring by Ushaidi in Kenya, for example, and in Kuwait, where women sent text messages to legislators to pressure them to vote for women's rights in the late 2000s; and the explosion of grassroots fundraising and "crowd-funding" by civic groups and political campaigns in which millions of small contributions can be raised through email solicitations and the use of the worldwide web, without the need to go through large intermediaries like NGOs and foundations.

The common theme in these examples is the value of horizontal organizing and communication, with little need for the kinds of bureaucratic, vertical forms of non-profits, political parties, newspapers, labor unions and other models from the past. Increasingly these models will be replaced by much more open, fluid and dynamic expressions of civic interaction, generating much more engagement and debate and thereby strengthening civil society in the process. Both the fabric of associational life and the health of the public sphere will improve dramatically, freed of the constraints that have held them back over the past hundred years. In the digital future imagined by these enthusiasts everyone will be connected, and everyone can participate. It's undoubtedly an attractive proposition, but is it true? Not according to the skeptics, who believe that civil society in the digital age harbors dangers as well as opportunities.

Thinkers in this camp like Morozov, Sherry Turkle, Jaron Lanier and others do not doubt the importance of social media to civic interaction, nor do they deny the benefits that can derive from the free and faster exchange of ideas and information.[29] But they do dispute the claim that these developments are unambiguously positive in their effects, and they reject the notion that there is anything inevitable about them, seeing politics and human agency as more powerful shapers of the future than technology. These thinkers also see the strengths of social media as potential weaknesses, depending on who uses them and how, and on whether or not they are complemented by face-to-face engagement and other, more traditional modes of civil society activity.

Take the speed and frictionless quality of virtual interaction, for example, which may not always be beneficial, just easier, giving rise to accusations of "clictivism," "slacktivism" and superficiality. You might follow me on Twitter but would you follow me to prison, like the adults and children who marched off to jail during the struggle for civil rights? Different forms of participation obviously imply different responsibilities, and they are likely to have different effects on those who practice them, a point that is made by those who fear that too much time spent on social media will reduce our capacity to connect with other people in real time. In fact the friction imposed by structure, hierarchy and slowing down may be extremely useful in revitalizing the public sphere, wherever filters are required to process information, test the validity of knowledge, bring excluded voices into the conversation or simply make a democratic decision – a frustration experienced by anyone who has participated in a social movement. There are already concerns that the sheer ease of search engines and other ICTs may be eroding incentives to undertake in-depth research, check facts and engage in actual conversation. "Once I was a scuba diver in the sea of words," writes Nicholas Carr; "now I zip along the surface like a guy on a jet ski,"[30] summarizing the fears of those who believe that only short-form arguments are now permissible in an era of declining attention spans – reduced to 140 characters or less in the case of Twitter.

Some digital enthusiasts do recognize the continuing importance of face-to-face engagement, though they see it as less exciting than social media and therefore less interesting to explore. This is understandable given the difficulties involved in bringing people together, especially from different backgrounds and where they disagree, as any community organizer will attest. But such direct interactions are essential to the processes of debate, deliberation and consensus-building that mark out the public sphere. Only when we agree to face each other physically are we forced to re-evaluate our own views and those of the person who is standing right in front of us. Otherwise a quick exit from the conversation is too easy. That's why no successful social movements (as opposed to social networks) are likely to be generated on the Internet, though all contemporary social movements use ICTs to organize themselves and communicate their message, just as movements in the past made use of the communications tools that were available to them at the time. And that's the crucial point: despite claims to the contrary, the Arab Spring and other episodes of protest did not come about because of Twitter, Facebook or cell-phones; they were organized by people who had the courage to make their feelings known in real, face-to-face encounters with those who opposed them. But it is certainly true that social media were useful tools in facilitating those interactions. Even so, research suggests that 93 percent of communications between activists in Cairo's Tahrir Square at the height of the protests were face-to-face. A separate sample revealed that only 13 percent took place on Twitter.[31]

In addition, the idea that social media can generate connections across different groups is not reflected in the reality of most digital engagement, which reflects a degree of Balkanization that mirrors the fractures and particularities we see in other, more traditional, structures of communication. MoveOn.org is a good example in the USA – highly effective at organizing supporters within the Democratic Party but completely ineffective at bringing other constituencies into the debate, so it is possible to be "wired but disconnected," at least from those with whom you disagree. As the web saying goes, "You'd be hard pressed to find a group on the Internet committed to the general common good."

Enthusiastic participation in like-minded groups on the worldwide web has not yet been translated into the development of public spheres that are capable of generating consensus about social and economic problems within or across societies where the views of citizens diverge.

Finally, it is important to remember that the Internet is not a free and open space. As noted earlier in this chapter, access is dependent on the private companies that own and control the servers and other systems that mediate all electronic communications, and where our data are stored, manipulated and controlled. A public sphere that is owned by a small number of private interests with their own commercial agendas to pursue is never going to be the liberating device that its enthusiasts would like to celebrate. But neither is it going to go away, in which case the most important question is not whether social media are good or bad for the public sphere but how best to utilize them in the future. This question releases us from sterile arguments between enthusiasts and skeptics and re-focuses the argument on how different forms of civic interaction can be successfully combined.[32] So what does the evidence tell us about this question? Can real and virtual conversation, organizing and debate be complementary, or must they displace one another?

Unfortunately the small amount of research that has been carried out to date on this question is not conclusive, though neither is it discouraging. Studies by the Pew Research Center's Internet and American Life Project published in 2011 suggest that there is a small but positive correlation between social media use by young people and other forms of civic engagement in the USA, including membership of a voluntary group and volunteering, and (less so) connecting with sources of "differing views."[33] These findings were confirmed by at least three other studies, though the samples used in all of them were small (between 2,000 and 3,000 respondents) and their methodologies were rather weak – consisting of self-reporting and public opinion surveys by telephone against a standard list of questions rather than detailed case studies with an evaluative dimension.[34]

Nevertheless, a number of civil society groups and networks are already demonstrating progress on the ground. Over half a million people signed a petition on Avaaz.org to clean up corruption in India in 2012, connecting with groups that successfully lobbied for changes in the legal framework through more conventional strategies on the ground, whether organized through the media, civil society pressure or politics.[35] Making Change at Walmart has developed a Facebook application that identifies which of your "friends" works for the company and then supplies them with information about the campaign and the rights they have as past or present employees.[36] And 350.org combines an online information bank on climate change with a national program of town-hall-style meetings with high-profile speakers such as Bill McKibben.

The lesson to be learned from these experiences is that online and offline action and communication must receive equal billing, unlike examples such as the "Kony 2012" viral video, which had very little presence on the ground. In addition, groups must work to preserve as much as possible of the communications infrastructure they utilize under democratic or collective ownership and control, in order to prevent the privatization and commercialization of the virtual public sphere. Open-source software is important here, but the "knowledge commons" also requires reducing our dependence on the physical infrastructure that is owned by corporate media.[37] The public spheres of the future will be ecosystems made up of many different elements (just like civil societies in general) – real, virtual and lots of combinations in between.

Conclusion

The long-term implications of these threats and opportunities are unclear, and they will continue to be contested. But there is no doubt that public spheres cannot operate effectively in protecting the common interest if communication, in the broadest sense, is privatized and segmented. Social institutions that support reason – by providing the producers of argument and ideas with both autonomy and connectivity – have to be protected. This is no idle quest, since protecting space for diversity while negotiating common rules and standards is perhaps the most important question facing humankind in the twenty-first century. If this question goes unresolved, further conflict is inevitable.

Although the theory of the public sphere explains much about civil society and its relationship to democracy and difference, it fails to explain how to deal with the structural factors that determine its effectiveness (such as inequality of voice), or how deliberation is converted into political decision-making, or how public engagement can be reinvigorated through different forms of associational life and communication. Like the other models explored in chapters 2 and 3, this one seems incomplete as an explanation of the challenges facing civil society, either as an idea or as a vehicle for social change. And if that is the case, what still remains to be done to unlock the mystery of the civil society puzzle?

5
Synthesis – Unraveling the Civil Society Puzzle

At this point in the argument it is customary to choose one model of civil society and terminate the debate. Either one takes the well-worn route of the revivalists or one trudges down the "road less traveled," ending up, after a few turns to the left, in the outer reaches of critical theory or searching for ways to combine state, market and civil society-building into a joint attack on social problems. The good news is that there is no reason to treat the civil society debate as a zero-sum game in which one model is accepted to the exclusion of the others, and every reason to embrace a holistic approach which integrates elements of all three schools of thought explored in chapters 2, 3 and 4. This is because civil society gains strength both as an idea and as a vehicle for social change when the weaknesses of one set of theories are balanced by the strengths and contributions of the others, a line of argument that enables us to focus on insights that lead to more effective action rather than worrying in the abstract about which theory is correct. In reality, each of these three perspectives has a great deal to offer.

Visions of the good society help to keep our "eyes on the prize" – the goals of poverty reduction, non-discrimination and the revitalization of democracy that, as chapter 3 explained, require coordinated action across many different institutions. Being clear about ends and means helps to guard against the tendency to promote certain institutions over others as a goal in and of itself – voluntary associations over states, for example, or markets over both. However, the vision of the good society says little about how such goals are going to be achieved, and associational life does seem to be an important – if incomplete – explanatory factor in most contemporary settings. As explored in chapter 2, structural definitions of civil society are useful in emphasizing the gaps and weaknesses of associational ecosystems that need to be attended to if they are to be effective vehicles for change. Earlier chapters also stressed, however, the differences and particularities of associational life that generate competing views about the ends and means of the good society. Without our third set of theories – civil society as the public sphere – there would be no just and democratic way to reconcile these views and secure a political consensus about the best way forward. Public spheres enable citizens to sort through their differences and achieve at least a functioning sense of the interests they hold in common so that they can be translated into norms, rules and policies that govern social and economic life. In turn, a healthy associational ecosystem is vital to the public sphere, since it is usually through voluntary organizations and the media that citizens carry on their conversations.

Each set of theories, then, is related to the others, but not, unfortunately, in any universal or easily predictable way. Although some theorists posit a direct transmission belt between associational life, positive social norms and the achievement of larger social goals, the evidence is very messy: every generalization has at least ten exceptions, and each lesson learned has at least ten qualifying conditions. Are associational life and the public sphere dependent or independent variables as they relate to the good society, or are they both depending on the circumstances? Are they "things" that can be factored into models or by-products of the interaction between politics, economics, culture, social structure and state-building as they operate through history? As the scale of inquiry increases from the local to the global, the number and range of intervening variables is certain to increase, making these questions more complicated still. What new light does the combination of these models shed on the civil society puzzle?

Associational life, the public sphere and the good society

In general terms many studies confirm that democratic consolidation is difficult to achieve without strong associational ecosystems and independent public spheres, because associations provide the channels or mediating structures through which political participation is mobilized and states are held accountable by their citizens, and public spheres provide the spaces through which civic action can be connected and scaled up. Mark Warren breaks down these "democratic effects" into three different categories: supporting public spheres of democratic engagement, encouraging the capacities of citizens for democratic participation and deliberation, and effects that underwrite democratic institutions through representation, legitimization and resistance.[1] The influence of popular movements in helping to overturn authoritarian rule across the world testifies to the importance of these effects even where associational life and the public sphere have been relatively weak. Whether democracy delivers other goals regularly identified with the good society – such as poverty-reducing growth and social inclusion – is not so clear cut. The short-term social and economic benefits of democratization have been disappointing in many countries, in which a failure to "deliver the goods" has led to disenchantment and reversal, but in the long run democracy is better at solidifying the social contracts and political coalitions that progress in these areas demands.[2] There is, at least, no evidence that the reverse is true – that the economic transformations required for developmental success necessitate authoritarian rule, even if certain countries have experienced such regimes during their transitions (compare South Korea, China and Taiwan, for example, with Botswana, Hong Kong and Mauritius). Recent research on "social capital" (which is not the same as associational life, though closely related) confirms that the strength, spread and connectivity of social networks do have an important influence in economic terms. World Bank research in Indonesia found that membership in local associations had a bigger impact on household welfare than did education, especially if their membership was socially heterogeneous and overlapped with membership in other groups. There is some evidence that these positive effects hold at the national level too, though this evidence is disputed.[3]

However, there are widely varying accounts of the transmission mechanisms involved in these relationships, with three schools of thought being particularly influential: the "civic culture" school sees associational life in general as the driving force behind the consolidation of the positive social norms on which the good society is built; the "comparative associational" school sees particular configurations of associational life as the key to securing the public policy reforms that give the good society its formal shape; and the "school of skeptics" disputes the links between "forms and norms" implied in either of these formulations, in favor of more complex interactions between different associational ecosystems and their context. The theory of the public sphere provides the "container" within which each of these schools of thought plays out in practice.

The civic culture school

The arguments of this first school of thought were explored in brief in chapter 2. According to their line of reasoning, "civic engagement" or "civic culture" – meaning a composite of associational life and voluntary interaction – are independent variables that provide societies with sturdy norms of generalized reciprocity (by creating expectations that favors will be returned), channels of communication through which trust is developed (by being tested and verified by groups and individuals), templates for collaboration (that can be used in wider settings), and a clear sense of the risks of acting opportunistically (that is, outside networks of civic engagement, thereby reinforcing cooperative behavior, or at least conformity with "civic values"). Assuming they are distributed broadly enough throughout the population, these positive social norms will produce a "society that is civil," and – assuming good people make good democrats – they will also create a constituency to support the social, economic and political reforms that are necessary to combat poverty and discrimination over time. The emphasis here is on generalized social capital, since, even if some of it is used for purposes defined as "bad," more will be used for purposes defined as "good," so the overall effect will still be positive. Scholars such as Putnam back up these hypotheses with reams of data that purport to show that "social capital" in the USA is declining (particularly traditional forms of civic and political participation) and that, as a result, America is heading for a crisis of social breakdown, political passivity and economic stagnation.[4] More recently, Putnam has extended his analysis to the impact of increasing ethnic and immigrant diversity in US cities, publishing results that claim to show that diversity tends to reduce solidarity and social capital, at least in the short term, a conclusion that runs counter to the rise of cross-ethnic community organizing and movement-building in diverse cities such as Los Angeles and New York.[5] Not for the first time, what the data purport to show and what people are actually doing on the ground seem very far apart.

Putnam's thesis, of course, is a great deal more nuanced and sophisticated than this brief summary suggests. Nevertheless, it has generated a large amount of criticism on empirical grounds (by those who question what has happened over time to different associations) and conceptual grounds (by those who claim that Putnam draws the wrong conclusions from data they accept). Others criticize the conflation of "civic" with "liberal-democratic" values (which makes associational life a transmission belt for norms that may be dominant, but not necessarily democratic) and the inversion of causes and effects – arguing that trends in social capital are dependent on factors outside of civil society, not the other way around. A common thread in these critiques is a question that connects Putnam and his colleagues to the second school of thought identified above: how can radically different forms of civic participation produce the same effects? If associational life varies as much as was described in chapter 2, then something magical must be happening to produce the generalized effects that Putnam predicts. The natural extension of this line of questioning is to claim that different associations do indeed have different influences, so the goals of the good society rest not on strengthening civic participation in general but on identifying which particular forms of participation are both lacking and important. In this sense, the key to the civil society puzzle lies through qualitative changes in associational life, not quantitative movements either "up" or "down."

The comparative associational school

One of the most influential writers in this second school of thought is Harvard academic Theda Skocpol, whose detailed historical studies in America have charted the shift from a civic world centered on locally rooted and nationally active membership associations to one centered on professional advocacy groups and social service providers that may have large numbers of supporters or clients, but not members in the true sense of the term.[6] The associations Skocpol mourns include the American Legion, labor unions (which claimed over 12 percent of all American adults as members in 1955), parent–teacher associations (PTAs, which claimed 9 percent), and a whole roster of organizations named for forest creatures such as elks, moose and eagles (sadly no one seems to have organized around frogs, bats or skunks). Because they represented a substantial cross-income and cross-interest social base (though predominantly white), these associations were able to form coalitions powerful enough to pressure the federal government into passing reforms that raised standards of health, education and welfare across America – for example, the GI Bill of 1944. As in successful developers later in time such as Kerala, West Bengal, Botswana and South Korea, associations like these constituted "highways" between government and citizens along which information and accountability could travel, and together they enabled citizens to develop a new sense of the common or public interest. Skocpol's research shows that such associations have declined dramatically in the USA since the Second World War – by 43 percent for the American Federation of Labor and Congress of Industrial Organizations (AFL-CIO), for example, 60 percent for the National Congress of PTAs, and 70 percent for the Masons.[7] The result is "diminished democracy" – an "advocacy universe that magnifies polarized voices and encourages class-biased policy outcomes."[8]

Why is the decline of such associations important? The first reason has already been mentioned – their success in pushing through broad-based welfare gains has been endangered by the collapse of cross-class, local-to-national bridges between civil society and government, as witness the failure of successive US administrations since the early 1970s to undertake any significant redistributive action. It cannot be coincidental that rising inequality and concentrated power in America have paralleled the decline of nationally federated associations such as labor unions and the gradual erosion of the public sphere described in chapter 4. We also saw in chapter 4 how – like rocks in a stream – engagement across interest groups in the public sphere can moderate extremist positions toward a political consensus on reforms, requiring overlapping memberships in different voluntary associations so that civil society can "escape any particular cage."[9] In addition, traditional associations tended to be financed through membership dues (not government contracts, philanthropy or foreign aid), which helped to keep members and leaders in close connection with each other, promoted accountability to a social base, and encouraged leadership development among low-income people instead of among elites claiming to act "on their behalf." And, since the skills of democracy are best learned through practice rather than in the class-room, by reading fundraising leaflets sent by mail or clicking a mouse on your computer, the increasing dominance of lobby groups and service-providing NGOs may threaten the norm-generating effects of associations by reducing citizen involvement to check- or letter-writing, web-surfing and attendance at the occasional rally – the "junk food" of par-ticipation, as Sidney Verba calls it.[10]

Similar arguments have been made in other contexts too. Community activists in both North and South argue that grassroots membership organizations that are internally inclusive and democratic are the key to civic life, since they encourage direct involvement by disenfranchised groups in economic and political processes and take on the structural barriers that limit equal participation and the equal distribu-tion of public benefits – groups such as the Community Farm Alliance in Kentucky, for example, the People's Rural Educa-tion Movement in Orissa, India, and the landless movement in Brazil.[11] By building voice, capacity and power from the bottom up, networks of such groups can influence the larger issues that affect them through policy advocacy and other forms of action in the public sphere that are simultaneously more effective, authentic and democratic. The Pushback Network in the USA is an excellent example.[12] Ashutosh Varshney's work on intercommunal conflict in Indian cities such as Ahmedabad suggests that one particular configura-tion of associational life – organizations that tie together the interests and activities of Hindus and Muslims – is the crucial factor in preventing outbreaks of inter-ethnic violence, and managing riots successfully when they do break out.[13] When associations are composed exclusively of one ethnic group then they cannot mediate in the interests of the whole (think Rwanda, Lebanon or the Balkans). But when organizations deliberately bring different groups together – for example, the neighborhood peace committees Varshney studied in his work – then negotiated settlements are possible.

The common theme of these studies is that the shape of associational life matters greatly in determining the influence of civil society on broader social goals, partly through effects on the health of the public sphere, and partly through effects on positive social norms. These are powerful arguments, but not, I think, conclusive. Varshney's work has been criticized by other scholars, who cite changes in industry and employment, migration and state responsibilities as just as important to the incidence of conflict in India as civic life per se.[14] The cross-constituency membership associations lauded by Skocpol and the grassroots groups praised by social activists are not guaranteed to secure the goals of the good society, especially if measured by the achievement of universal rights. As she herself admits, the great protest movements of the 1960s for civil and women's rights did not fit her model, since, although new membership associations were vital – examples included the Southern Christian Leadership Council and the Student Non-Violent Coordinating Committee – such movements were driven forward by a combination of grassroots protest, radical activism and professional lobbying, not by traditional cross-interest associations such as PTAs and the American Legion. And although whites did play a role in the civil rights movement, the movement was overwhelmingly African-American in character, just as the women's movement was driven by women, and the gay rights movement was driven by gays, lesbians and queers. The fact that all three movements achieved substantial gains shows that associations that represent a particular constituency can be just as effective in achieving the goals of the good society, if not more so – unless, perversely, equal rights are not included. Citing 205 cases of socially progressive legislation passed by the US Congress between 1963 and 1991, Jeffrey Berry concludes that the growth and influence of "citizens' lobby groups" based in Washington, DC, is good for democracy and the public interest. "These are not thin citizens," he says, "but full-bodied activists, and the nation needs more of them, not less."[15] People who join such groups are more likely to participate in other aspects of the political process (including voting) and be members of other groups where they do more than write a check – helping to produce those overlapping memberships that all schools of thought have seen as crucial. The problem lies not with the rise of public-interest lobbying but with the fact that such groups empower only some parts of the US population. Equally, many traditional membership associations fought not for broad-based social reforms but for narrow concerns such as gun ownership (the National Rifle Association grew dramatically when it allied itself with partisan politics in the 1970s) and the prevention of abortion (by the National Right to Life Committee, founded in 1973).

The school of skeptics

These qualifications have been elaborated in great detail by my third school of thought, which consists of writers who accept that the structure of associational life and the public sphere are shifting in important ways to suit a rapidly changing context, but deny that these shifts have any a priori consequences. In part, this is because new routes to participation and communication are expanding even while older ones are in decline. *Pace* Putnam ("kids today just aren't joiners"), soccer clubs, community organizations, immigrant and self-help groups, churches, Internet-based activism, alternative labor networks and the environmental movement are exploding, and many of these newer associations – which Skocpol dismisses as professional lobbyists – do have large numbers of members (the Sierra Club, for example, or the National Organization of Women).[16] Some – such as the American Association for Retired Persons – also involve them in activities beyond check-writing, and even in organizational governance. So, while the decline of traditional associations may have some negative consequences, they may be offset by the rise of new forms of organizing. Changing patterns of civic life may simply reflect a necessary reordering so that civil society remains a positive force as circumstances change. But is this true?

In the USA at least, the evidence suggests that new patterns of associational life may be adding value in certain areas but that they cannot substitute for large-scale, face-to-face engagement across geography and politics, so in this sense Skocpol's analysis is correct. Take the example of so-called "alt(ernative)-labor" groups such as the Restaurant Opportunities Center and the National Domestic Workers Alliance in the USA. Both have succeeded in organizing and protecting workers (often undocumented immigrants) who have been difficult for the AFL-CIO to reach, but their impact tends to be limited to short-term gains in wages and working conditions, which are at risk in the future because the labor force remains officially non-unionized. Such groups are also staffed by professionals and funded by donors from outside the communities that are being organized, so they may not develop the democratic leadership and accountability structures that have been crucial to the success of civil society in the past.[17] A similar pattern is emerging in the online–offline organizing groups that were analyzed in chapter 4: short-term gains in advocacy and campaigning but little sign that the ongoing structures of citizen organizing are being strengthened on the ground. This is important because much of the impact of associational life on politics and public policy has been dependent on sustained engagement across the civil-political divide. But clearly it is too soon to reach any firm conclusions about the influence of these changes in the civil society ecosystem.

Following this line of argument, one would not expect any necessary correlation between the characteristics of associations and their effects, a reality that is recognized even by the godfathers of compassionate conservatism such as John Dilulio, former director of the White House Office of Faith-Based and Community Initiatives. "We do not know," he says after reviewing ninety-seven rigorous studies of faith-based civic associations and their work, "whether America's religious armies of compassion . . . necessarily out-perform their secular counterparts."[18] Research by scholars in the USA such as Deborah Minkoff, Nina Eliasoph and both Mark Warrens (yes, there are two of them, each working separately on civil society and politics) shows that contentious organizations regularly foster norms of democracy and cooperation, since when people secure their rights and entitlements they become more willing to collaborate with others.[19] And, arguing from the opposite direction, research also shows that social service groups and volunteering can have a positive effect on civic and political activism on the larger stage.[20] Increasing numbers of non-profit organizations are hybrids that combine elements of advocacy, service provision, capacity-building and political action – they are rarely "one thing or the other." "Congregations," as David Campbell puts it, "are not just contractors but sites and resources for church based coalitions and organizing networks" that play an increasing role in politics as well as service.[21] But for this to happen, groups must make strong links *outside* their congregations and constituencies, develop an open and self-reflective culture, and make a reality of what Eliasoph calls "empowerment talk" throughout their operations.[22] Only then can voluntary associations act in and expand the public sphere, reaching out to forge broader alliances around contentious issues which otherwise would be frozen in polities that are permanently polarized.

The most detailed interrogation of the "forms and norms" debate comes from Nancy Rosenblum, who finds that the effects of associational life on the moral dispositions of their members, and hence on the health of democracy, are complex, fluid and often surprising.[23] Associations that are often dismissed by neo-Tocquevillians – such as self-help and identity-based groups or street gangs of young people – may have important democratic effects, since, even though their members, resembling Narcissus, may talk only about themselves, at least they take turns in doing so, learning in the process a little of the reciprocity that underpins cooperation and active citizenship. This is an important observation, given that such self-help groups (for example, Alcoholics Anonymous and Weightwatchers) had over 25 million members in the USA in 1996.[24] Anti-democratic groups can have positive effects on democratization (such as, for some analysts, the Serbian Resistance Movement in Kosovo), and pro-democratic groups can harm it, as the Independence 99 movement may have done in the Czech Republic.[25] Associational cultures are diverse and often contradictory, but they may still produce important benefits by articulating neglected voices in the public sphere or developing new loyalties and capacities among their members. Some small groups have the same problems as large bureaucracies (think dysfunctional families) while others show strong commitments to internal democracy, equity and self-criticism. Only "hate groups," Rosenblum concludes, are unambiguously negative in their effects.

Therefore, the ideal of civic associations as "mini-democracies" is not essential to the argument that democracy and the public sphere depend on a vigorous associational life. It follows that legislation to enforce internal structures and characteristics in line with standard criteria is unlikely to be effective – accountability to a social base, for example, or democratic elections for their leaders. Encouraging such qualities may be desirable, but attempting to enforce them may, as Hannah Arendt once observed, be the beginning of a slippery slope to "totalitarianism as the end point of unremitting congruence."[26] This is an uncomfortable conclusion for civil society enthusiasts, since it implies that associations can practice undemocratic or discriminatory behavior – such as a refusal to hire gay employees – and still qualify as members. Is the preservation of civil society as a protected zone of pluralism a more important objective than enforcing universal standards in a society that is civil? The public sphere must decide the answer to that question, in court if necessary, as it did when the US Supreme Court forced the Minnesota Jaycees to accept women members in 1984.[27]

Outside the USA, this debate is much less well researched, and contexts are more varied. As we saw in chapter 2, this makes it difficult to draw conclusions, but those studies that do exist suggest a similarly complex picture. Different forms of association, or associations with different characteristics, may have similar effects, and the factors that seem to mark out "high performers" – such as flexibility, accountability and learning – are shared by successful public and private sector institutions too. A Ford Foundation study of civil society and governance across twenty-two developing countries in 2001 found that associational life does contribute to democracy and state accountability, but not as much as was thought, and only when certain conditions are met – alliances and coalitions between associations in the public sphere, for example, inclusive membership, and independence, including as much domestic funding as possible.[28] "Values-based" NGOs in developing countries do not automatically perform more effectively, since performance depends on the contexts in which they operate and the goals of the work they do – different organizational structures and characteristics are required, for example, to operate effectively in service provision, policy advocacy and capacity-building. A clear vision or mission, a balance between economic development and political empowerment, strong vertical and horizontal linkages to draw in resources and connect poor people to public and private institutions, and the multiplier effect of strengthening people's own capacities and leadership are common denominators, but they may not be achievable in authoritarian settings or where resources are in short supply. Even if they are, research in Asia and Latin America has shown that "we cannot say *a priori* that any one type of organization is inherently more or less responsive to, or representative of, the needs of the rural poor."[29] Where the empowerment of underrepresented groups is top priority, building membership-based, internally democratic associations into social movements is likely to be crucial, but in other contexts more traditional forms of organization may be more important. As in the case of the USA described above, it is not the presence or extent of associational life that makes the difference by itself, but the character of pluralism and the actual activities of different types of association as they are shaped by history and contemporary context. As a good illustration of this conclusion, take the example of civil society at the global level.

Global civil society

If the links between associational life, the public sphere and the good society are so complex at the national level, what hope is there for constructing a satisfactory synthesis across national borders? The literature on global civil society has expanded enormously since 2000, with some authors claiming that this phenomenon heralds a major shift in international affairs.[30] Yet despite the achievements of global campaigns on land mines, conflict diamonds, debt relief and other pressing issues, world politics remains stubbornly state-centric, and many questions have been raised about the legitimacy and effectiveness of global citizen action. Approaching these questions from a tripartite approach to civil society yields significant dividends, because it allows us to evaluate the characteristics of transnational associations, the goals they pursue, and the global public spheres in which they operate both separately and together. Many analyses confuse or conflate these three dimensions, producing recommendations that are overly romantic, misleading or unworkable, yet it is clear that problems in the structure of transnational associational life and the weakness of the global public sphere make it much more difficult to realize the goals of the good society at the global level.

Theories of global civil society rest on the assumption that increasing numbers of problems are transnational in nature, requiring global solutions that will be more effective and legitimate if they incorporate democratic principles of participation and accountability (think climate change, humanitarian intervention and the regulation of international finance). Increased civil society participation, protest, pressure and proposal-making can strengthen the moral standing of international decisions; increase the likelihood that governments will ratify new treaties and legal obligations; improve the content of global policies and policy debates; strengthen implementation, monitoring, and public education on the ground; and inject charismatic leadership into international affairs. The world is unlikely to be governed by a global state at any time in the foreseeable future, but multi-layered, multi-actor "networked" governance structures are already in operation, and they are growing by the day. Examples include the World Commission on Dams, the Global Alliance for Vaccines and Immunization, the Kyoto Protocol, and the Make Poverty History campaign.[31] Over 3,400 civil society groups took part in the World Summit on the Information Society in Geneva in 2005, lobbying successfully for the inclusion of public interest concerns in regulations governing the Internet, just as a broad alliance coordinated by the World Federalist Movement had built public and political support for the International Criminal Court seven years before.[32] These examples remove one immediate objection to global civil society (that it cannot work since no global government exists) but raise another set of questions about the feasibility of citizen participation at the global level when there are so many different interests in play and so few satisfactory structures to accommodate them in the world of international institutions.[33]

The structure of transnational associations is central to these questions, since it is clear that a "level playing field" does not yet exist. Attention and support may go to those who shout loudest or have the most aggressive marketing departments, not necessarily to the most effective or democratic groups.[34] "Global" alliances are dominated by voices from the North, where civil society groups have the resources and political access to articulate their demands. Global civil society will be stronger and more authentic when it makes room for trade unions, international social movements, networks of academics and professionals, and local civil society organizations that link with their counterparts across national borders, becoming less NGO-centric in the process. Indeed, some of the most promising manifestations of global civil society are not those that showcase the "big names" in international advocacy such as Oxfam or Greenpeace, but horizontal networks of associations representing large numbers of low-income people acting collectively both at home and in the corridors of international power. Shack/Slum Dwellers International, for example, already has hundreds of thousands of members from thirty-three different countries.[35] This is an important way of addressing a common problem in global civil society, namely the tendency for international associations to develop self-generating agendas for advocacy and action, de-linked from realities and interests on the ground. As Sidney Tarrow has pointed out, the most effective transnational activists are "rooted cosmopolitans," "people who grow up in and remain closely linked to domestic networks and opportunities" even while they extend their activities into the international arena.[36] A study of civil society participation in global conferences undertaken by the United Nations Research Institute for Social Development found that, although international policies did shift a little as a result, the most important benefits were often domestic in nature because that is where most pressure could be exerted on legislation, and where civil society alliances and coalitions could be strengthened.[37] The most successful examples of global civil society's potential impact are those where these questions have been explicitly addressed – for example in the NGO Coalition on the International Criminal Court, in which a substantial number of groups from Africa and Latin America participated.[38]

The second structural problem in global associational life is accountability. Who, if anyone, do NGOs represent, or are they just special-interest groups that wear a friendlier disguise? Who enjoys the benefits and suffers the costs of what global campaigns achieve, especially at the grassroots level? Who speaks for whom in a global coalition, and how are differences resolved when participants vary in strength and resources? Whose voice is heard when conflicts are filtered out in order to communicate a simple message? And how are grassroots voices mediated by institutions of different kinds – Northern NGOs and Southern NGOs, Southern NGOs and community groups, and so on down the line? Traditional ways of addressing these questions are not feasible in networked governance, because there is no single, hierarchical authority to which accountability can be addressed, and no obvious way of using electoral mechanisms given that most civil society groups are not formally representative of a constituency. This dilemma has been used as a device to deny legitimacy to NGOs in recent years, but worries about "lack of representation" are often misplaced, since civil society organizations *supplement* formal democracy by contributing their *voices* to global debates, not their *votes*.[39]

Faced with these problems, the best way forward is to experiment with multiple accountability mechanisms that balance the needs of different stakeholders (through peer review, for example, or mutually agreed rights and responsibilities) and to support different ways of aggregating civil society voices without pretending that the results can ever be perfect. Options range from simple solutions that are already in operation in the international system (the "Arias Formula," for example, which allows civil society groups to provide input to UN Security Council deliberations in their areas of expertise), through more formal mechanisms that give those most affected a seat on the governing body of international institutions (such as the Global Fund for HIV/ AIDS), to new ideas such as a Global Civil Society Forum (constituted from national umbrella bodies and international NGO coalitions), a UN Peoples' Assembly (first suggested by Richard Falk and Andrew Strauss in 1997), a global "e-parliament" (designed to connect civil society groups and elected officials through electronic debates), and global political parties that might be fashioned around such existing entities as the International Democratic Union and the Global Greens.[40] Clearly, all these ideas require a major leap of faith as well as a lot more concrete experimentation, but that has never been a barrier to civil society action.

The deficiencies of transnational associational life create obvious problems for the idea of a "good global society," because the normative visions of some civil society groups might dominate those of others – not just because of North–South power differentials but because of more basic differences in values and objectives. Early work on global civil society tended to assume that all transnational associations were like-minded in their support for a unified vision of social and economic transformation, a world without war, and reforms in international relations based on greater democracy, equality and respect for international law. These assumptions were incorrect, and more recent research has documented a number of arenas in which major differences exist, including international religious coalitions, debates about arms control, and attitudes toward intervention in Iraq, Afghanistan, Libya and Syria. The most comprehensive of these accounts have been developed around the emergence of the "globalized Christian Right" and the pro-gun lobby in international forums. After the Beijing Conference on Women in 1995, domestic groups such as Focus on the Family and Concerned Women for America in the United States began to build links with Catholic, Mormon and Muslim allies in other countries to advance a conservative social policy agenda in the United Nations on issues such as abortion, women's rights and human cloning, and they have had some success in influencing international policies around reproductive health and HIV/AIDS.[41] In similar vein, the National Rifle Association has spearheaded a global effort to build support for the right to bear arms, acting as an adviser to domestic civil society groups in Brazil, Australia and elsewhere in their own efforts to resist gun control and pulling together an international advocacy coalition called the World Forum on the Future of Sport Shooting Activities, which opposes the views of the International Network on Small Arms at the United Nations and elsewhere.[42]

Some commentators see these as examples of "uncivil society," but in reality they are simply groups with different views, and they have the same rights as anyone else to promote their positions in the global public sphere.[43] After all, if contentious politics produces better solutions at the national level, there is no reason to think otherwise when views collide across national borders, assuming that all of them have an equal chance of being heard. There are no empirical data to substantiate the actual size of conservative networks like these, but there is some evidence from global opinion polling to show that despite political differences, shared values are emerging on issues such as globalization, inequality, climate change and democracy.[44] There is also evidence that those who regularly cross these borders develop more cosmopolitan values and attitudes toward global governance, so perhaps global citizen action can strengthen "global citizenship" even if those citizens continue to disagree with each other on some detailed policy questions.[45] Even so, the key issue is surely the need to develop more "global public spheres" to sort through these differences and find more consensus, not to pretend that they will disappear as a "natural" consequence of globalization. Such differences will grow as more civil society associations from a wider range of countries gain in strength and begin to exercise their voice on the international stage. Mohammed El Sayed-Said, for example, sees global civil society as a platform for dialogue between Islamists and secularists across and beyond the Middle East, while John Dryzek has articulated a whole theory of "deliberative global politics" designed to moderate in conflicts across national borders when formal institutions fail.[46]

The problem, of course, is that these global public spheres are very weak, fractured by unequal access, constrained by the commercialization of the international media and barriers relating to copyright and censorship, and penetrated by governments intent on identifying communications between those who threaten national security or who represent threats of other kinds.[47] Websites such as openDemocracy, Wikipedia and OneWorld provide the beginnings of an international communications infrastructure that enables groups with different views to engage with each other across national borders, and advances in information technology make this task significantly easier. The Symbolic Systems Program at Stanford University, for example, is experimenting with "online environments for democratic deliberation" that use the worldwide web to support sophisticated transnational communications far beyond the limitations of conventional email, list-serves and bulletin boards, while a video-communications bridge between the World Economic Forum and the World Social Forum has also been tried out, so far without success.[48] As in other experiments with web-based communications at the national level, clear advances have been demonstrated in terms of information storage and exchange, collaboration, publishing, intelligence-gathering and mobilizing groups with similar opinions, but much less so in terms of connecting communities with divergent or conflicting views.[49]

Some see the World Social Forum itself as a potential global public sphere, though it collects together only those on the left of global politics. It certainly provides a space for free engagement among substantial numbers of people (there were 109 forums in 2004, attracting hundreds of thousands of participants, as compared to five in 2001), and it has resisted strenuous attempts by some of its leaders to impose a focus on particular policies and positions, in favor of continued open dialogue.[50] It retains its accessibility to poorly resourced grassroots groups and social movements, and for this reason alone forms an important component of global civil society, but neither the World Social Forum nor any of the other innovations on offer provides much more than a suggestion of what might be possible in a global public sphere. Therefore it is not surprising that global civil society has had a limited impact on the problems it seeks to address. In its present form, it is clearly not a substitute for democracy in global governance, but it will grow stronger as each dimension of civil society connects with the others at the international level. "Global civil society is diverse, creative and chaotic. That's what makes it always interesting, often unpredictable, and sometimes very powerful."[51]

Conclusion: is any generalization possible

Let me offer four preliminary generalizations abou[t]
between associational life, the public sphere an[d]
society at different levels. First, the nature of
depends on how one envisions the goals of the [?]
or, more precisely, the means by which these g[?]
ized in practice. The "civic culture school" see[s]
social norms as the driving force behind broade[r]
and associational life in general as the medium
these norms are strengthened. The "comparati[ve]
school" sees specific policy changes as the [?]
society, supported by mechanisms in the p[?]
enable the necessary political coalitions t[?]
Certain forms of association will be i[?]
reforms, while others may be irrelevant
so, say those in the "school of skeptics
know in advance whether any sort of
likely to produce the effects these oth
this line of reasoning, the best that can
as much freedom, capacity and socia[?]
and let civil society sort the rest out

On closer inspection, these three
not mutually exclusive, since the g[?]
are most likely to be achieved when
for all associational life is combine[d]
associational forms that are missing [?]
ecosystem. So my second generalization is that i[?]
system that matters, not the characteristics of its individua[l]
components. Overlapping memberships, cross-interest coalitions, hybrid organizations, and the appropriate mix of
bonding and bridging, grassroots groups and intermediaries,
advocates and service providers are more likely to make
associational life a handmaiden of broader social progress.
Some kinds of association will be crucial to political accountability, but not to trust and cooperation, while others may
encourage positive social norms but have little impact on

countervailing structures of authority can introduce increasing reciprocity into the general constitution of a society in
which serious asymmetries exist. Calls to "participate more"
often ignore the economic difficulties that strip people on
low or insecure wages of the time and energy to do precisely
that, especially when privatization, in the absence of a welfa[re]
state, shifts ever greater burdens onto voluntary associati[ons]
families and women. If people feel exploited by the [?]
nomic systems in which they work, ignored by the [?]
systems in which they vote, and excluded by socia[l]
that discriminate by race, gender or sexual orien[tation]
not surprising that "exit" often seems a better [?]
"voice." Economic segregation in labor and ho[using]
separates citizens from one another and ma[kes]
alliances much more difficult to cement, jus[t]
structure of work makes organization and [?]
ing much more difficult. This may be [?]
current wave of democratization in m[?]
producing redistributive progress of [?]
movement would do more to re[?]
in earlier waves after 1945. Henc[e]
amount of moralizing about th[?]
is easy to forget that women p[?]
voluntary associations in t[?]
because they were disenf[?]
sphere, or that it took th[?]
mize attempts by volun[?]
for political equality, [?]
tion. These conditio[?]
a supportive conte[?]
by civil society a[?]
in the broader [?]
are the depen[?]
An inte[?]
ments o[?]
both a[?]
alone[?]

dn[?]
tural pr[?]
tionalized co[?]
of universal rights [?]

good society – is incomplete. Side by side, there is at least a chance that their strengths and weaknesses can be harmonized, and that all three can benefit from a positive and conscious interaction. An inclusive and well-articulated associational ecosystem can be the driving force of the good society, but the achievements of the good society are what make possible the independence and level playing field that underpin a democratic associational life. Without a functioning public sphere neither would be possible, since there would be no space for associations to operate in defining the good society's ends and means. This is just as true at the global level, where states remain the duty-bearers of international treaties, transnational networks are essential to enforce compliance, and global public spheres are required to foster debates about international norms. An integrated approach like this should enable the design of interventions that are more likely to be effective, since – rather than isolating particular parts of the puzzle and failing to see where the other pieces fit – all the relevant factors can be addressed collectively, and in some rational order. What might that mean in practice?

6
So What's to be Done?

In most cases, asking civil society scholars to distil policy and practice from their theories is akin to seeking help on plumbing from the local vicar. An embarrassing silence, followed by the sound of shuffling feet, is the usual response to the obvious question – so what should we *do*? Those who do attempt an answer to this question fall into moral exhortations about improved personal behavior (a typical response from the "civil society revivalists"), romantic assumptions about community- or movement-building (especially common on the left), or – worst of all perhaps – a series of recommendations based purely on what the author thinks the donors and the politicians want to hear. The result is usually an anemic shopping list made up of NGO capacity-building, boot camps for better citizens, and calls to return to some imaginary past where people were nicer to their neighbors and the land flowed with milk, honey and bridging social capital. Robert Putnam's book *Bowling Alone* closes with a long list like this, couched in almost evangelical tones: "So I set before America's parents, educators . . . and young adults the following challenge . . . that bridging social capital will be substantially greater than it was in their grandparents' era," a task guaranteed to set the pulse racing among teenagers nationwide. It doesn't seem to have occurred to the good professor that "America's parents" are already confronting such challenges on a daily basis, but in contexts where they get no help from employers or the state, and often little from each other.[1]

In any case, "what to do" depends on what one understands civil society to be. Devotees of associational life will focus on filling in the gaps and disconnections in the civil society ecosystem, promoting volunteering and voluntary action, securing an "enabling environment" that privileges NGOs and other civic organizations through tax breaks, and protecting them from undue interference through laws and regulations that guarantee freedom of association. Believers in the good society will focus on building positive interactions between institutions in government, the market and the voluntary sector around common goals such as poverty reduction, human rights and deep democracy. Supporters of civil society as the public sphere will focus on promoting access to, and independence for, the structures of communication, extending the paths and meeting grounds that facilitate public deliberation and building the capacities that citizens require to engage with each other across their private boundaries. Those who see civil society as an independent variable will try to build it directly, while those who see it as a by-product of other forces will try to manipulate them in order to produce the best outcomes overall. And if, like me, you see virtue in all these approaches, then the logical thing to do is to look for interventions that can strengthen the interactions between different models that were described in chapter 5 in order to generate *an inclusive associational ecosystem matched by a strong and democratic state, in which a multiplicity of independent public spheres enable equal participation in setting the rules of the game*. An integrated approach like this avoids the tendency to substitute voluntary action for state-building or the demands of democratic politics.

The problem is that this approach is also the most complicated for policy and practice, defying any attempt to find a "magic bullet" (such as more volunteering), and implying measures that are always specific to their time and place. So the more rigorous we are about the civil society debate, the more we return to familiar but intractable problems of culture and history, state–society relations and the material bases of change. And the deeper we delve in this way, the more difficult it becomes to settle on easy answers on what to do, when, and where. This produces a level of uncertainty – and requires a level of flexibility – that sits uneasily with the drive for quick results measured against certain pre-defined criteria that motivates donor agencies in the world of philanthropy and foreign aid. "Civil society-building" is really a "black box," implying interactions between all sorts of variables in an ever-changing context, which make associa-tional life and the public sphere a handmaiden of broader changes in social, economic and political structures, and vice versa. Chapter 5 shed some light on how these interactions work in theory, but in practice they are almost impossible to manufacture. Underlying these complexities is the thorny issue of whether intervention of any sort can lead to predict-able outcomes, since the more contingent its development, the more difficult it will be to ensure that civil society leads to any particular ends. The easiest things to influence (such as the number of NGOs in society) are generally the least important, while the most important – such as a commitment to a common life – are the least amenable to change. And because civil society has many different faces, Mr Hyde may be the result even where Dr Jekyll is the objective.

Where does this frightening image leave us? I think there are two things that can be done to nurture civil society without falling into reductionism or false universals. The first is to strengthen the preconditions for effective interactions between associational life, the public sphere and the good society by attacking all forms of inequality and discrimina-tion, giving people the means to be active citizens, reforming politics to encourage more participation, guaranteeing the independence of associations and the structures of commu-nication, and building a strong foundation for institutional partnerships, alliances and coalitions. The second is to support innovations in associational life that encourage citizen action to operate in service to the good society through the public sphere. Instead of returning to the patterns of a bygone era, this requires the reinvention of associational life to suit the radically different circumstances of today. If these actions are successful, there is a chance that civil societies will be able to shape themselves organically over time. The outcomes may not conform to a single, prior definition, but they will be more sustained and effective.

Building the preconditions for a true civil society

A consistent theme in the argument thus far has been the inability of associational life to cement the foundations of the good society by itself. Only a deeper commitment to equal citizenship and democratic self-government can bring the two together through the consensus-making functions of the public sphere. Remember that the success of each of our three models of civil society is dependent on its interaction with the others. If these interactions are to operate effectively, there are certain things that have to be done almost regardless of the context, focused on the structural barriers that undermine the conditions in which such synergies can develop. Chief among those conditions are poverty and inequality, which remove the support systems people need to be active citizens and deprive them of the security required to reach out and make connections with other people.

It may seem perverse to argue that legal protection of equal rights and the provision of jobs with decent wages, adequate help with childcare, fair taxation, access to quality health and education services and a comprehensive social safety-net are interventions aimed at civil society-building, but this is precisely what they are, since in their absence both associational life and the public sphere are likely to be dominated by elites. Inadequate access to childcare and early childhood education, for example, has been cited as the most important factor underlying lower civic participation rates among women in

the United States than in Western Europe.[2] Guaranteeing
these things to all citizens is one of the best ways to ensure
that they have the capacities and opportunities required to
shape civil society in accordance with their own wishes,
rather than those of donors, governments or corporations.
Unfortunately, governments usually do the opposite by
attempting to "force-feed" civil society development through
special programs against the background of widespread inequality and insecurity. Britain's "Big Society" is a classic
example of this reversal of priorities, attempting to strengthen
citizen participation by funding social enterprises, public–
private partnerships and the devolution of responsibilities,
but in the middle of a recession and budget cuts that are
destroying many people's ability to participate.[3]

The persistence of serious inequalities endangers civil
society as a democratic enterprise. The sharing of space and
resources between Christian and Jewish congregations in
Manhattan that I cited in chapter 4 works, in part, because
both are made up of reasonably affluent participants. It is not
too difficult to live a cosmopolitan life from a position of
privilege and safety, since the risks involved are minimal and
the effort required is less intense. But expecting people on
the breadline to share, participate and cooperate as equals is
unreasonable unless this is the safe and rational thing for
them to do. Arguing about politics, and holding power to
account, takes both energy and courage, especially when
politics and power decide to fight back.

No doubt "reasonable people will disagree" on the best way
to provide safety, security and equal protection throughout
society, and the appropriate mix of state, market and voluntary action that these goals require, but it is difficult to see
how, by themselves, either government, business or non-
profit groups could achieve the desired results. Institutional
complementarity is essential. This requires that a careful
watch be maintained over the effects of privatization and
commercialization on civil society in each of its three disguises. Support for "co-production" – the joint provision of
public goods and essential services by the state, firms and

community groups working together – creates synergy in the management of local resources and increases a sense of ownership over the results. Seattle, for example, has a Neighborhood Matching Fund through which public and community resources can be pooled, mirroring experiments throughout urban Latin America which give citizens public and private support for their initiatives as well as a role in the budget process and other aspects of governance.

In addition to these interventions, governments have the responsibility to guarantee the independence of associational life and the public sphere, which is necessary to their roles in promoting transparency, accountability, dialogue and debate. This is best done through legal protection of civil and political rights, especially rights of information, association and free speech, and by establishing an enabling environment for citizen action and the independent media which is composed of a judicious mix of fiscal and regulatory structures that can balance freedom with accountability. In practice, most environments fail this test, being overly intrusive and controlling of associational life, especially in authoritarian contexts where the temptation to co-opt citizens' groups and the means of communication is almost irresistible. Even in mature democracies like the USA these temptations are apparent, especially in the security environment that has followed in the wake of the terrorist attacks of September 11, 2001.

In this climate, government intrusions can always be used to target groups for political or ideological reasons, which is anathema to a healthy civil society in which different views and voices have a right to be expressed. We saw in chapter 3 how different schools of thought approach the question of "uncivil society," meaning the existence of associations whose purposes and practices may offend one group or another. There are many ways to deal with this problem, but legislating for "congruence" – a state-sponsored definition of acceptable behavior – runs the risk of freezing out more radical voices. A "concordat" between government and the voluntary sector is more effective, laying out their reciprocal rights and responsibilities and backed up by a mix of legal measures and voluntary codes of conduct. Such concordats are already being tried out in the UK, Canada and elsewhere. It is especially important that citizens can join and leave non-profit groups as easily as possible, since this makes overlapping memberships – whose importance has been emphasized throughout this book – more likely.

In terms of the public sphere, the free flow of information is essential for equal opportunity, consensus-building, and the ability of citizens to hold government and business accountable for their actions. Making access to information about finance, employment and legal rights widely available helps to offset the isolation of excluded groups, and renders it more likely that public policies can be influenced in their favor. Therefore, public information disclosure laws and a dense network of public media and communication channels are priorities, along with more genuinely public spaces of every sort. They may be physical spaces (such as markets and squares, community centers and public libraries, especially if they have free Internet access), virtual spaces (rolling back the increasing commercialization and centralized control of the Internet's architecture and codes by a small number of corporations), educational spaces (building up public universities at the expense of private education) and spaces in the media (through support to community radio, public television, subsidized cable channels and a diverse and pluralistic press, including newspapers and magazines published in vernacular languages). Governments can play their part here by regulating the communications industry in the public interest – for example, by preventing companies from buying up local radio stations en masse, insisting that cable companies finance community access centers as a condition of their franchise, and subsidizing the satellite costs of public service broadcasting.

In addition, public engagement needs paths and meeting grounds where people can form friendships, challenge each other and forge new alliances and loyalties across their particularities. In Belarus, the Polish Stefan Batory Foundation is supporting a series of round-table meetings designed to facilitate dialogue between government, business and non-profit groups about future directions in society – an obvious but unprecedented step in an authoritarian context like this. Mixed schools, colleges and housing projects; joint media ventures; collective production and marketing organizations such as cooperatives; and the co-management of natural resources by different groups – all of these things build bridges across the lines of class and ethnicity and help to cement new senses of the "public."

More broadly, realizing the positive synergy between our three models of civil society requires reforms in both representative and participatory democracy in order to revitalize the public sphere, recognize that associations have a legitimate (non-partisan) role to play in the political system, and strengthen the links between citizens and their governments. These are all ways of cementing the relationships that connect associational life to the decision-making processes that shape the good society. In terms of the formal political system, the fact that 50 percent of eligible voters declined to participate in the 2012 US presidential election is understandable if politics is seen as corrupt, ineffective and unrelated to ordinary people's concerns.[4] But the answer to this dilemma is to clean up politics via campaign-finance reform, election monitoring and improved voter registration and voting procedures, not to provide more escape routes, through volunteering and the like, from political engagement. Part of this process has to be the devolution or decentralization of political authority (backed by the necessary fiscal and financial resources) so that citizens can share in the control of all matters except those where higher-order action is necessary to ensure a fair distribution of power, interests and resources. Bolivia's Law of Popular Participation is a rare effort to institutionalize subsidiarity in this way, and one which has been instrumental in efforts in that country to reverse the privatization of municipal water supplies. Expanding citizen voice, participation and representation in state decision-making generates consensus, trust and social learning; greater accountability and responsiveness in state institutions; and more protection for minority rights and interests.

Civil society has been a major beneficiary of the rise of participatory and deliberative democracy since the early 1990s, and making more space for direct participation in the processes that surround formal politics is an important part of any agenda for the future. Deliberative opinion polls, alternative voting procedures and modes of representation, facilitated debates on major policy dilemmas, and opening more spaces for citizens to be heard are all important, though obviously dependent on a supportive political context. Classic forms of participation (such as town-hall meetings) may be too costly and time-intensive for today's busy citizens – as Morris Fiorina points out, they were originally "welcome diversions" from a long and lonely New England winter, after the harvest and before the fields were ready to plough.[5] So new forms of participation, perhaps arranged around the workplace or facilitated by information technology, are especially important. At root, any increase in participation is welcome, since we learn to be citizens not through books or training but through experience and action.

Promoting stronger ties between civic and political activity in these ways is a risky business, carrying with it the dangers of co-optation and loss of independence, but we saw in chapter 2 why these ties need to operate successfully if political life is to be truly democratic and effective in securing a consensus on good society reforms – democratization cannot occur without real politics. However, there is no consensus on how the two spheres connect. Some of the most promising routes are "non-party politics," increased civil society advocacy and policy work, separating civic and political action into different parts of the same association or network, electing or appointing civil society activists into government positions, and support for party systems as opposed to particular political parties. There is some evidence that donor support in these areas has become more sensitive over time.[6] There is empirical evidence for and against the proposition that "civic education" (which is especially popular in schools, among the politicians if not the pupils) leads to greater involvement in politics and volunteering over time. But other things being equal, those who participate in voluntary associations are more likely to participate in politics, especially if they do so at school and university.[7]

Where does all this leave us in terms of our agenda for civil society action? Civic education, community service and expanded modes of informal political participation can certainly be useful, so long as they are not state-controlled or used as a substitute for reforms in formal politics. These measures can help to build the preconditions for effective interactions between associational life, the public sphere and the good society, but they rely on capacities and connections among associations that must also be developed. And that, as we shall see, is just as difficult a task.

Facilitating the development of a healthy associational ecosystem

If associational life and its effects are as complicated as described in previous chapters, then any attempt to influence them through foreign aid, philanthropy or government intervention will be replete with difficulty and danger. Yet the approach of the civil society-building industry that has proliferated since 1989 – with some exceptions – resembles a crude attempt to manipulate associational life in line with Western, and specifically North American, liberal-democratic norms: pre-selecting organizations that donors think are most important (advocacy NGOs or other vehicles for elites, for example, usually based in capital cities), ignoring domestic expressions of citizen action that do not conform to Western expectations (such as informal, village- or clan-based associations in Africa and the Islamic world, more radical social movements or pre-political formations), spreading mistrust and rivalry as fledgling groups compete for foreign aid, and creating a backlash when associations are identified with foreign interests. The creation of public spheres is usually ignored, apart from occasional support for independent media groups and organizations promoting government accountability. And ignoring Ralf Dahrendorf's warning that "it takes six months to create new political institutions, six years to create a half-way viable economy, and . . . sixty years to create a civil society," project timescales are collapsed to bite-sized two- or three-year chunks and accountability is reoriented up the system to outside donors and regulators.[8] Nurturing civic institutions takes careful and sensitive accompaniment over long periods of time. By contrast, the aid industry resembles a bulldozer driven by someone convinced that they are heading in the right direction, but following a map made for another country at another time. The Coalition Provisional Authority's insistence that Iraq needed a Ministry of Civil Society in the chaos that emerged after the US occupation is a good example of priorities gone horribly awry.[9]

In the West, voluntary associations may be less vulnerable to the vagaries of aid agencies but they are still exposed to the dangers of dependence on government contracts and the whims of private foundations and other donors. This can easily distort the authenticity of pluralism by favoring some groups over others with large financial and technical support, retarding the development of embedded relationships between citizens and their associations, and contributing still further to state retrenchment and privatization. It is not difficult to start up new NGOs (unless one lives in Myanmar or maybe China), a task that fits comfortably with the donor agencies' tendency to focus on the short term and the easily measurable, or to invest in the physical infrastructure of the non-profit sector. But, by themselves, these interventions do little. They are not genuine attempts to facilitate the evolution of organic patterns of associational life, but misguided attempts to shape their destiny according to predetermined norms – what Xiarong Li calls "civil society determinism."[10] The results are unlikely to be successful. Like the unhappy offspring of a dysfunctional marriage, their future as independent, self-sustaining entities will always be under threat. External support can be useful as the oil that lubricates the engine of associational life, but it can never substitute for the hand that drives the car.

A range of independent evaluation studies confirms this gloomy prognosis, but why is the record so poor?[11] Donor agencies are rarely held accountable for the impact of their decisions. If they were, fewer mistakes would be made. These are not unreasonable demands, one might think, but they are shockingly absent from the world of philanthropy and foreign aid. In addition, external agendas are often contradictory, with support for political associations in pushing for democracy offset by support for economic associations pushing for market liberalization (or, at the organizational level, support for NGO service provision trumping support for advocacy and popular mobilization). While the donors stated their support for "pluralism" in Bosnia after the Dayton Accords, what they actually sought out and funded was "cheap service delivery," according to evaluator Ian Smillie.[12]

Official aid is tied to the political agendas of the administration in power, so it would be naive to expect an attitude of pure detachment in an area as politicized as civil society funding, and steps are already being taken to reduce the potentially damaging effects of outside help through increased donor coherence and coordination.[13] Nevertheless, evaluations of the US-supported "Greater Middle East Initiative," for example, civil society assistance in Russia and Ukraine, and aid to NGOs and social movements in India all show strong distortions due to an overinvestment in NGOs with weak grassroots links.[14] This is not to say that there have been no successes. George Soros's efforts in Eastern Europe (from providing photocopiers for dissidents to launching independent grant-making bodies such as the Stefan Batory Foundation) have been notable, as have some of the efforts of other foundations and international NGOs. Similar claims have been made for the "color revolutions" in Ukraine, Georgia and Kyrgyzstan between 2003 and 2005, though in all three instances there were also criticisms of outside (and specifically US) support for elements within civil society that lacked local legitimacy, and that may have contributed to ongoing political instability and democratic reversal. These problems have been a constant feature of foreign aid to civil society, with intense bursts of activity prior to and following the first round of democratic elections followed by a much harder struggle to sustain and deepen democracy – a pattern that has also been observed in older contexts such as Spain and Poland, and contemporary processes such as the Arab Spring.[15] The best results come when outside efforts support a local movement that is already well organized and has a very specific objective. In this scenario, small amounts of money and technical assistance at the right point in time can make a major difference.

If the record is so poor, what can be done to improve it? The first rule of thumb is always to look for forms of associational life that "live" relatively independently in their context – not just the "usual suspects." They may be conservative-minded mosque associations in Lebanon (which Samir Khalaf shows are contributing to the development of tolerance), burial societies in South African townships (which played key social, economic and political roles under apartheid) or labor unions in France and Brazil (which have been prime movers in the burgeoning global justice movement).[16] It is groups like these that occupy the frontiers in organizing new responses to problems of community and association against the background of globalizing capitalism, resurgent nationalism, and the fragmentation they breed. And if, as scholars have demonstrated convincingly, associational life was radically reshaped in the West at the end of the nineteenth century by urbanization, industrialization and immigration, then it can be reshaped again. The global justice movement has been particularly innovative in developing new and less hierarchical structures, practices and organizing techniques across borders, though it remains to be seen whether these innovations will generate any consensus at the level of specific policy alternatives.

Second, we should focus on the associational ecosystem by fostering the conditions in which all of its components can function more effectively, alone and together. If the "soil" and the "climate" are right, associational life will grow and evolve in ways that suit the local environment. This requires support for as broad a range of groups as possible, helping them to work synergistically to defend and advance their visions of civic life, providing additional resources for them to find their own ways of marrying flexible, humane service with independent critique, and leaving them to sort out their relationships both with each other and with the publics who must support them, and to whom they must be accountable, if their work is to be sustained. Support for civic–political linkages in associational life is also important, including the advocacy role of non-profit groups and their ability to marry different functions together as recommended in chapter 5 – the creation of hybrid organizations that combine service delivery, capacity-building and advocacy, or the combined personal and structural changes captured in the civil rights movement's philosophy of "the love that does justice." "Service politics" might be considered an oxymoron by some, but it is worth consideration in its ability to pull these two dimensions of citizen action together.[17] Regulatory regimes and the contractual arrangements used by governments when they fund non-profit organizations need to be sensitive to this balance. It is the depth and continuity of this ecosystem that enable citizens to resist authoritarian takeovers and respond to new political opportunities when they arise.

Other important measures include support for less visible associations and those representing the interests of marginalized groups (especially women's associations, which have been proven to be better intermediaries between people and institutions in many contexts);[18] renewing the pipeline of leadership in order to address the tendency of associations to develop greater inertia and self-interest over time; and strengthening the connections that link people vertically and horizontally into new relationships and networks for collective action across in-group boundaries, whether in broad-based coalitions and alliances, social movements, or more basic relationships between intermediary organizations and membership groups with some social constituency. All these measures will increase the influence of less powerful groups on public policy as well as building overlapping relationships and accountabilities.

Third, we should focus as much attention as possible on strengthening the financial independence of voluntary associations, since dependence on government contracts, foundations or foreign aid is the Achilles' heel of authentic civic action. Resources always have a steering effect that must be factored into questions of organizational identity, function, mission and accountability. Associations that have a diverse revenue base rooted in local contributions are usually better able to resist pressure from donors, keep their sights firmly on their core mission, and dispel the accusation that they are simply pawns of outside interests. This does not mean replicating traditional models of charity fundraising developed in the West (the "starving baby" syndrome), but encouraging a much broader set of mechanisms, including member dues, cost-recovery for services provided, commercial income, foundation grants, endowments and the kind of democratic self-funding models described at the end of chapter 3. Despite some scandals (for example, the senior executive at the Markle Foundation in New York who visited Fifi La Roo's spa in the Hamptons on "official business"), foundation funding remains important, at least in theory, because of its flexibility and long timescales, though as we saw in chapter 3, the rise of "philanthrocapitalism" may erode these strengths because of its control-orientation and desire for short-term measurable results of certain kinds.[19] Supporting locally endowed, independent grant-making foundations such as the Dalit Fund in India or community foundations across the world is an especially useful thing to do because it devolves responsibility and resources away from distant bodies like the Gates or Ford Foundations. National and subnational development funds (in which different donors pool their resources) also offer promise.[20]

Finally, because so little is known or understood about civil society in non-Western contexts, further research on the realities and complexities of associational life across the world is extremely important. More research will not lead to more effective assistance by itself, but it will create a better repository of information on which donors can base their judgments, and make it easier to expose and challenge the assumptions they often make. In short:

- be clear and transparent about why you are promoting certain patterns of associational life, and take responsibility for the results;
- focus on the conditions in which associations can shape themselves and their relationships, not a predetermined view of which forms you think are most important;
- think of associational life as an ecosystem and look for components that are weak, absent or disconnected;
- provide resources for as broad a range as possible of groups to come together and articulate their own visions of the future; and
- promote indigenous roots and accountability as the key to effective resource generation, independence and effectiveness.

Conclusion

How large does an idea have to be before it qualifies as a "big idea"? Does civil society count, or is it too complex and restricted in its relevance to certain contexts, cultures and periods in history? Civil society, in the ways I have explored it in this book, is certainly an important idea, because it helps us to understand and change the world simultaneously. But since there is no consensus about what civil society is, what it does, or even whether it exists in certain parts of the world, it would be foolish to make too many claims of this kind. What seems certain is that civil society will continue to provide an important framework for action and debate long into the future.

As I hope I have shown, civil society is simultaneously a goal to aim for, a means to achieve it, and a framework for engaging with each other about ends and means. When these three "faces" turn toward each other and integrate their different perspectives into a mutually supportive framework, the idea of civil society can explain a great deal about the course of politics and social change *and* serve as a practical framework for organizing both resistance and alternative solutions to social and economic problems. Theories of the good society help to keep our gaze on the goals and challenges that motivate the search for freedom and human progress; theories of associational life help to explain how to meet those challenges through the medium of non-state action, which is always necessary but never sufficient; and theories of the public sphere connect the two together by providing a framework for argument and negotiation around social goals and the strategies required to meet them. Many of the difficulties of the civil society debate disappear when we lower our expectations of what each of these schools of thought has to offer in isolation from the others, and abandon attempts to enforce a single model, consensus or explanation.

Building a true civil society in all three ways will take enormous energy and imagination, and this is why the inspiration that this idea provides to popular struggles is so important. At the Djibouti Peace Conference for Somalia in 2000, the language of civil society was used extensively by local forces as a counterpoint to continued rule by local warlords.[21] "What right do you have to take away a concept that we find so important in our work?" was the comment made to me by an activist in India in 2002, and quite right too. Whatever its theoretical shortcomings, civil society does offer a touchstone for social movements, and, because the essence of civil society is collective action – in associations, through the public sphere and across society – this debate reminds us that individual efforts and experiences can never substitute for the relationships of love, solidarity, sacrifice and friendship that are the essence of our true human nature. At a time when such relationships are severely strained by broader changes in society, international relations and the economy, this may be the most important lesson that civil society has to teach.

It is a truism that civil society is what we, as active citizens, make it, but it is also true that "social energy," or "willed action," is the spark that ignites civil society as a force for positive social change. The determination to do something because it is the right thing to do, not because we are told to do it by governments or enticed to do it by the market, is what makes associational life a force for good, provides fuel for change in the practices of states and business, and motivates people to raise their voices in the public sphere. In this sense civil society is a story of "how people use imagination, resilience and conviction," as Paul Hawken puts it, "to perform daily miracles in redefining our relationship to the environment and one another."[22] While criticisms of civil society are often valid, think what the world would be like without the dreams of the good society, the resources of voluntary associations and the arguments of the public sphere. Life would certainly be less interesting without the Raging Grannies of Montreal, Cat Lovers Against the Bomb, Drop Yer Drawers (a charity in Texas that distributes free underwear), Citizens Against Breast-Feeding (not one of my personal favorites) and the Grand Temple Daughters of the Elk. Against the background of weak democracies, strong bureaucracies, corporate power, legalism and nationalism resurgent, civil society is essential to the prospects for a peaceful and prosperous world order in the twenty-first century, because it "leads us to a renewed awareness of the fusion of the moral, the social and the political in the constitution of all human communities."[23]

The daily struggles of millions of civil society groups across the world provide a useful reminder that mass action on the basis of human community may yet generate the foundation for alternative forms of politics and a new kind of society. In this conviction, at least, I am happy to be called a "civil society revivalist." At its best, civil society is the story of ordinary people living extraordinary lives through their relationships with one another, driven forward by a vision of the world that is ruled by love and compassion, non-violence and solidarity. At its worst, it is little more than a slogan, and a confusing one at that, but there is no need to focus on the worst of things and leave the best behind. Warts and all, the idea of civil society remains compelling, not because it provides the tidiest of explanations but because it speaks to the best in us, and calls on the best in us to respond in kind.

Notes

PREFACE

1 http://www.google.com/trends/explore?hl=en-US#q=civil
   %20society&cmpt=q; last accessed June 24, 2013.
2 Ehrenberg (2011: 15)
3 http://www.google.com/trends/explore#q=social%20media
   &cmpt=q; last accessed June 24, 2013.
4 http://www.google.com/trends/explore#q=social%20
   entrepreneur&cmpt=q: last accessed June 24, 2013.

CHAPTER 1   INTRODUCTION – WHAT'S THE BIG IDEA?

1 From an undated fundraising letter signed by Cato Institute
   president Edward H. Crane and received by the author in
   2001. The incentive for contributors was a complimentary
   copy of *Little Civics Lessons* by P. J. O'Rourke.
2 The quotes in this section come in the order they are written
   from Eberly (1998: 4–5); the Advocacy Institute's 2001 annual
   report; Scholte (2002: 2); Boggs (2000: 259); Stephen White,
   cited in Post and Rosenblum (2002); Seligman (1992); and
   Rifkin (1995: 280). See also Eberly (2008).
3 Hann and Dunn (1996: 1); Chambers and Kymlicka (2002:
   1); Khilnani (2002: 11); and Seligman (1992: 169).
4 The late Gordon White (1994: 376).

5 See, for example, Seligman (1992); Keane (1998); Ehrenberg (1999); Foley and Hodgkinson (2002); Hall and Trentmann (2005); Alexander (2006); and Edwards (2011a).
6 Ehrenberg (1999: xi).
7 For a good review of these debates, see Cohen and Arato (1992).
8 See the contributions to Post and Rosenblum (2002) and Chambers and Kymlicka (2002).
9 The best summary of these critiques is Edwards et al. (2001).
10 Foley and Hodgkinson (2002: xix).
11 Chambers (2002: 94).
12 Chambers and Kymlicka (2002: 8); Cohen (1999); Keane (1998); Alexander (2006).
13 Bellah (1995: 277).
14 See Edwards (1999a) and Acemoglu and Robinson (2012).
15 Salamon (2010: 187).
16 See, for example, Harbeson et al. (1994); Keane (1988); Escobar and Alvarez (1992); and Fox and Hernandez (1992).
17 Edwards (2000b: 10).
18 Wolfe (1998: 18).
19 The conversation was reported to me by Professor James Manor of the Institute for Development Studies at the University of Sussex.
20 Chandoke (2003); Rieff (1999).
21 Edwards (2000b); Van Rooy (2004); and Jordan and van Tuijl (2006).
22 Available at http://www.edelman.com (2002).

CHAPTER 2   CIVIL SOCIETY AS ASSOCIATIONAL LIFE

1 Goody (2002: 157).
2 From Engel's foreword to Adams (1986: viii).
3 O'Connell (1999: 125).
4 De Tocqueville (1945: vol. 2, 114).
5 http://www.nfpa.org/research/statistical-reports/fire-service -statistics/us-fire-department-profile (2012).
6 Cited by Adams (1986: 160).
7 Cited by Reilly (1995: 7).
8 Walzer (1998: 124).
9 Post and Rosenblum (2002); Uphoff (1993).

10 Salamon (1993); Mathews (1997).
11 Data from OneWorld South Asia: http://Southasia.oneworld.net/news/india-more-ngos; and International Center for Not-for-Profit Law (2013).
12 Xiaoguang (2002).
13 BRAC at a glance: www.brac.net.
14 Data from United States Department of State (2012); National Council of Voluntary Organizations (2012).
15 Gottesdiener (2012).
16 Lichtenstein (2002).
17 Skocpol (1999, 2003).
18 Andersen et al. (2006); Dekker and Van Den Broek (2005).
19 Anheier et al. (2012: 19).
20 Skocpol (1999).
21 Cohen and Arato (1992: x).
22 *The Economist*, January 13, 2001: 42.
23 Antlov (2003).
24 Read and Pekkanen (2008).
25 Lewis (2008).
26 See Foley and Edwards (1996).
27 Hashemi (1997).
28 Ramesh (2007).
29 Edwards (2010).
30 Walzer (1998); Lasch (1996); Cohen and Arato (1992: viii).
31 Edwards (1999a: 94); Varshney (2002); Peters and Scarpacci (1998).
32 See Smith (2000); Chen et al. (2007).
33 De Oliveira and Tandon (1994: 73).
34 Woolcock (1998); Edwards (2000a).
35 Hawken (2007).
36 Warren (2001b); Bebbington (1996); Patel et al. (2001); Chetkovich and Kunreuther (2006); Pushback Network (2008); Lichterman (2005).
37 Tarrow (2012).
38 *Chicago Sun Times*, November 5, 2002; GPN activists mailing list, November 15, 2002.
39 See Tarrow (1998); Giugni (1999).
40 Skocpol and Williamson (2012).
41 Van Gelder (2011).
42 See Tilly and Tarrow (2007); Hawken (2007).
43 Gottesdiener (2012); Eidelson (2013).

44 INCITE (2007); Choudry and Kapoor (2013); Dauvergne and LeBaron (2013).
45 Dawson (2001); Harris (1999).
46 Howell and Pearce (2001); Nosco (2002); Metzger (2002); Unger (2008).
47 See Aslan (2005a).
48 Gellner (1994: 103).
49 Hassan (2012).
50 Kienle (2012).
51 Kandil (1995); Salam (2002); Hawthorne (2004); Paya (2004); Bamyeh (2005); Ezzat (2005); Khallaf and Tur (2007).
52 Hassabo (2007); Beinin and el-Hamalawy (2007).
53 Shaaban (2007).
54 See Mardin (1995); Ibrahim (1995); Kelsay (2002); Azra (2002) Zubaida (2002); Bayat (2007); and Beinin and Vairel (2009); White (1996).
55 Aslan (2005b).
56 Muasher (2011).
57 Tamman (2008); An-Na'im (2008).
58 Bayat (2007); Kelsay (2002).
59 Mamdani (1996).
60 Orvis (2001); Hearn (2001); Lewis (2002).
61 Bayart (1986); Bratton (1994); Harbeson et al. (1994); Mamdani (1996); Comaroff and Comaroff (1999); Lewis (2004).
62 Lehman (2008); Obadare (2011).
63 Sogge (2006).
64 Abe (2005).
65 Obadare (2011).

CHAPTER 3   CIVIL SOCIETY AS THE GOOD SOCIETY

1 "Thoughts of the First Accused: Saad Eddin Ibrahim to the Supreme State Security Court, 29 July 2002, case number 13244."
2 Roepke (1996); Cornuelle (1965).
3 Seligman (2002: 28); Hall (1995); Keane (1988); Gellner (1994).
4 Cited in Myers (1996: 53); Perez-Diaz (1993).
5 Lewis (2004); Seckinelgin (2004).

6   Edwards (2007).
7   http://www.seasonsfund.org (2007).
8   Hawken (2007).
9   Heinrich (2008).
10 http://www.grantspace.org/Tools/Knowledge-Base/Funding
    -Resources/Individual-Donors/American-giving (2011).
11 Cited by Seligman (1992: 2).
12 Walzer (1998: 132), though the emphasis is mine.
13 A term used by McClain and Fleming (2000) to refer to the
    work of Putnam, Etzioni and others.
14 Rosenblum (1998: 350).
15 Putnam (2000). This anecdote comes from Constance Bucha-
    nan, a former colleague at the Ford Foundation, who used to
    work at the Harvard Divinity School. The emphasis is mine.
16 Keane (1998: 45).
17 Galston and Levine (1998: 36).
18 See Robin (2001).
19 Uvin (1998); Salem (1998); Majed (1998); Khalaf (2002).
20 The most recent investigations of the Columbine shootings
    cast doubt on this finding.
21 The origins of this remark lie in Fareed Zakaria's review of
    Francis Fukuyama's book *Trust* in the *New York Times*, cited
    in Levi (1996).
22 Chambers (2002).
23 Geremek (1992); Berlet and Lyons (2000).
24 Keane (1998: 50).
25 Seligman (1992: 197–8).
26 Verba et al. (1995: 457, 2012).
27 Howell (2005); Hagemann et al. (2008); Coffe and
    Bolzendahl (2011).
28 Fowler and Biekart (2008).
29 Zadek (2001).
30 Carter (1999: 230).
31 Edwards and Post (2008: 4).
32 Bishop and Green (2008); Nicholls (2011); Bugg-Levine and
    Emerson (2011).
33 Cited in Edwards (2010: 57).
34 Pamela Hartigan, cited in Edwards (2010: 74).
35 Hirschman (1970).
36 Frumkin (2006).
37 Rodriguez (2007); Hall and Perry (2013).

38 See Edwards (2010: 70); Weisbrod (2004).
39 Eikenberry and Kluwer (2004).
40 For details of the organizations described in this section see Edwards (2013).
41 Cited in Reilly (1995: 8). The second quote comes from Rick Cohen, former executive director of the National Committee on Responsive Philanthropy in Washington, DC.
42 Post and Rosenblum (2002: 3, 8).
43 Cited by Keane (1998). The second quote comes from Rieff (1999: 12).
44 On Kerala, see Heller (1996); Harris (2001). On state–society synergy more broadly, see Evans (1996); Tendler (1996); Edwards (1999a: ch. 3).

CHAPTER 4   CIVIL SOCIETY AS THE PUBLIC SPHERE

1 Cited in Chatterjee (2002).
2 Rosen (2001: 75).
3 McClain and Fleming (2000: 303).
4 Keane (1998).
5 Keane (1998: 169).
6 http://www.opendemocracy.net (2013).
7 Avritzer (2002).
8 Avritzer (2002); Fung and Wright (2003); Boyte (2004); Leighninger (2006); Levine (2007).
9 Boyte (2004: xi, 2008); Schattan et al. (2010).
10 Mutz (2006); Barker et al. (2012); Lohmann and Van Til (2012).
11 Cited in McConnell (2003: 41). See also Hampshire (1999).
12 Etzioni (1993: xi).
13 Howell and Pearce (2001: 237).
14 Arendt, cited in Myers (1996: 4); Walzer (1998: 303).
15 Jordan (1992: 197).
16 Personal communication with John Keane.
17 See Peklo (2004).
18 Eliasoph (1998); Guinness (2008).
19 Marquand (2004: 2).
20 See, for example, Boggs (2000); Bollier (2001); Lessig (2001); Benkler (2007).
21 Global Partners and Associates (2007).

22 *Guardian* (2013).
23 Bollier (2001).
24 Lessig (2001); Levine (2002); Benkler (2007).
25 Cited in Douglas and Borgos (1996: 25).
26 Edwards and Foley (2001: 139).
27 Shirky (2008, 2010); Castells (2012); Johnson (2013); Schmidt and Cohen (2013).
28 Morozov (2013).
29 Morozov (2011, 2013); Lanier (2011, 2013); Turkle (2011).
30 Carr (2008); Bauerlein (2008); Farrell (2006).
31 Fuchs (2012: 14).
32 Lentz (2011); Berkhout and Jansen (2012); McChesney (2013); Eliasoph (2013).
33 Pew Research Center's Internet and American Life Project (2011).
34 Georgetown University Center for Social Impact Communication (2011); Christensen (2011); Kahne et al. (2013).
35 www.avaaz.org/en/highlights.php (2013).
36 Bloch (2012).
37 Lievrouw (2011); Shah and Jansen (2011).

CHAPTER 5 SYNTHESIS – UNRAVELING THE CIVIL SOCIETY PUZZLE

1 Warren (2001a).
2 Isaac (1998).
3 Grootaert (1999); Pritchett and Kaufman (1998).
4 Putnam (2000).
5 Compare Putnam (2007), for example, with Wang and Winn (2006) and Pushback Network (2008).
6 Skocpol (1999).
7 Skocpol (1999: 475).
8 Skocpol (2003); Fiorina (1999: 20).
9 Hall (1995: 15).
10 Verba et al. (1995); Fisher (2006).
11 Edwards (1999b); Chetkovich and Kunreuther (2006); Chen et al. (2007).
12 Pushback Network (2008).
13 Varshney (2002).
14 Van der Veer (2002).
15 Berry (1999b: 389); see also Berry (1999a).

16 Putnam (2000: 15); Ladd (1999); Ray (2002).
17 Gottesdiener (2012); Eidelson (2013).
18 From the preface to Johnson (2002: 6).
19 Warren (2001a); Warren (2001b); Minkoff (2002a, 2002b); Eliasoph (2013).
20 Meyer and Hyde (2004); Lichterman (2005); Building Movement Project (2006); Henriksen and Svedberg (2010).
21 Campbell (2002: 208).
22 Eliasoph (2011).
23 Rosenblum (1998, 1999); Post and Rosenblum (2002).
24 Wasserman (1999: 240).
25 Kopecky and Mudde (2007).
26 Cited in Post and Rosenblum (2002: 16).
27 See Galston (2002).
28 http://www.ids.ac.uk/idsproject/civil-society-and-governance -programme. See also Blagescu and Court (2007).
29 Bebbington and Thiele (1993: 21); Edwards and Hulme (1995); Edwards (1999b).
30 Edwards and Gaventa (2001); Keane (2003); Kaldor (2003); Batliwala and Brown (2006); Walker and Thompson (2008); Jordan (2011); Dryzek (2012).
31 Benner et al. (2004); Slaughter (2004).
32 Hill (2008); Glasius (2008).
33 Anderson and Rieff (2005).
34 Bob (2005).
35 Patel et al. (2001); Edwards (2001).
36 Tarrow (2005: xiii).
37 Pianta (2005); UNRISD (2005).
38 Glasius (2008).
39 Edwards (2000b); Jordan and van Tuijl (2006).
40 Edwards and Zadek (2003); Van Rooy (2004); Widener Law Review (2007); Strauss and Falk (1997); Sehm-Patomaki and Ulvila (2006); Scholte (2008); Thompson (2008).
41 Butler (2006).
42 Morton (2006); Bob et al. (2007)
43 Khagram and Alvord (2006).
44 Price (2007).
45 Mau et al. (2008).
46 El Sayed-Said (2005); Dryzek (2006); Alexander (2006).
47 Albrow and Glasius (2007).

48 Davies et al. (2004).
49 Surman and Reilly (2003).
50 Glasius and Timms (2005); Whitaker et al. (2005).
51 Glasius et al. (2006: v).
52 Warren (2001a).
53 Edwards and Sen (2000); Edwards and Post (2008).
54 Tilly (2007: 188).
55 Ehrenberg (1999: 249).

CHAPTER 6   SO WHAT'S TO BE DONE?

1   Putnam (2000: 404).
2   Andersen et al. (2006).
3   Edwards (2011b).
4   http://elections.gmu.edu/voter_turnout.htm (2013).
5   Fiorina (1999).
6   Carothers (2006).
7   Giugni (1999); Galston (2001); Edwards and Foley (2001); McFarland and Thomas (2006); Levine (2007); McBride and Sherraden (2007).
8   Cited in Keane (2003: 159).
9   Encarnacion (2011).
10 Li (1999).
11 Sampson (1996); Van Rooy (1998); Carothers and Ottaway (2000); Howell and Pearce (2001); Jenkins (2002).
12 Smillie (1996: iv); Hulme and Edwards (1997).
13 Advisory Group on Aid Effectiveness (2008).
14 Hawthorne (2004); Senzai (2004); Jalali (2005); Henderson (2003); Lutsevych (2013).
15 Carothers (2006); Beissinger (2006); Forbrig and Demes (2007); Encarnacion (2011).
16 Khalaf (2002).
17 The term "service politics" comes from Long (2000).
18 See the papers by Bebbington and Carroll, Salmen and Reid, and Uphoff and Krishna, all in the World Bank Social Capital Library of works in progress at http://www.worldbank.org/poverty/scapital/index.htm (2013).
19 Rutenberg (2002). On "philanthrocapitalism," see Edwards (2010).

20 The model of consolidated development funds is explored in Edwards (1999a: ch. 7).
21 Lewis (2002).
22 Hawken (2007: 5).
23 Hann and Dunn (1996: 3).

References and Bibliography

Abe, C. (2005) 'Reinventing development and the test of civil society in Africa', *CODESRIA Bulletin*, nos. 3 and 4, 70–2.

Acemoglu, D., and J. Robinson (2012) *Why Nations Fail: The Origins of Power, Prosperity and Poverty*. New York: Crown Business.

Adams, J. L. (1986) *Voluntary Associations*. Chicago: Exploration Press.

Advisory Group on Aid Effectiveness (2008) *Civil Society and Aid Effectiveness: Synthesis of Findings and Recommendations*, http://web.acdi-cida.gc.ca/cs.

Albrow, M., and M. Glasius (2007) 'Democracy and the possibility of a global public sphere', in M. Glasius, M. Kaldor and H. Anheier (eds), *Global Civil Society 2007/8*. London: Sage.

Alexander, J. (2006) *The Civil Sphere*. Oxford: Oxford University Press.

An-Na'im, A. (2008) *Islam and the Secular State: Negotiating the Future of Shari'a*. Cambridge, MA: Harvard University Press.

Andersen, R., J. Curtis and E. Grabb (2006) 'Trends in civic association activity in four democracies: the special case of women in the United States', *American Sociological Review*, 71 (June), 376–400.

Anderson, K., and D. Rieff (2005) 'Global civil society: a sceptical view', in M. Glasius, M. Kaldor and H. Anheier (eds), *Global Civil Society 2005/6*. London: Sage.

Anheier, H., M. Kaldor and M. Glasius (2012) 'The Global Civil Society Yearbook: lessons and insights 2001–2011', in M. Kaldor, H. Moore and S. Selchow (eds), *Global Civil Society 2012: Ten Years of Critical Reflection*. Basingstoke: Palgrave Macmillan.

Antlov, H. (2003) 'Not enough politics! Participation and the new democratic polity in Indonesia', in E. Aspinall and G. Fealy (eds), *Indonesia: Decentralization and Democratization*. Singapore: Institute of South-East Asian Studies.

Aslan, R. (2005a) *No God but God: The Origins, Evolution and Future of Islam*. New York: Random House.

Aslan, R. (2005b) 'From Islam, pluralist democracies will surely grow', *Chronicle of Higher Education*, March 11.

Avritzer, L. (2002) *Democracy and the Public Space in Latin America*. Princeton, NJ: Princeton University Press.

Azra, A. (2002) 'The challenge of democracy in the Muslim world: traditional politics and democratic political culture', keynote address to the Conference on the Challenges of Democracy in the Muslim World, Jakarta, March 19–20.

Bamyeh, M. (2005) 'Civil society and the Islamic experience', *ISIM Review* (spring), 40–1.

Barker, D., N. McAfee and D. McIvor (eds) (2012) *Democratizing Deliberation: A Political Theory Anthology*. Dayton, OH: Kettering Foundation Press.

Batliwala, S., and L. D. Brown (eds) (2006) *Transnational Civil Society: An Introduction*. Bloomfield, CT: Kumarian Press.

Bauerlein, M. (2008) *The Dumbest Generation: How the Digital Age Stupefies Young Americans and Jeopardizes our Future*. New York: Penguin.

Bayart, J.-F. (1986) 'Civil society in Africa', in P. Chabal (ed.), *Political Domination in Africa*. Cambridge: Cambridge University Press.

Bayat, A. (2007) *Making Islam Democratic: Social Movements and the Post-Islamist Turn*. Stanford, CA: Stanford University Press.

Bebbington, A. (1996) 'Organizations and intensifications: campesino federations, rural livelihoods and agricultural technology in the Andes and Amazonia', *World Development*, 24 (7), 1161–77.

Bebbington, A., and G. Thiele (eds) (1993) *NGOs and the State in Latin America*. London: Routledge.

Beinin, J., and H. el-Hamalawy (2007) 'Egyptian textile workers confront the new economic order', *Middle East Report*, March 25.

Beinin, J., and F. Vairel (2009) *Workshop on Social Movements in the Middle East and North Africa: Shouldn't We Go a Step Further?* Florence: Robert Schuman Center for Advanced Studies, European University Institute.

Beissinger, M. (2006) 'Promoting democracy: is exporting revolution a constructive strategy?', *Dissent* (winter), 84–9.

Bellah, R. (1995) *Habits of the Heart: Individualism and Commitment in American Life.* Berkeley: University of California Press.

Benkler, Y. (2007) *The Wealth of Networks: How Social Production Transforms Markets and Freedom.* New Haven, CT: Yale University Press.

Benner, T., W. Reinicke and J. M. Witte (2004) 'Multisectoral networks in global governance: towards a pluralistic system of accountability', *Government and Opposition*, 39 (2), 191–210.

Berkhout, R., and F. Jansen (2012) 'Introduction: the changing face of citizen action', *Development*, 55 (2), 154–7.

Berlet, C., and M. Lyons (2000) *Right-Wing Populism in America.* New York: Guilford Press.

Berry, J. (1999a) *The New Liberalism: The Rising Power of Citizen Groups.* Washington, DC: Brookings Institution Press.

Berry, J. (1999b) 'The rise of citizen groups', in T. Skocpol and M. Fiorina (eds), *Civic Engagement in American Democracy.* Washington, DC: Brookings Institution Press.

Bishop, M., and M. Green (2008) *Philanthrocapitalism: How the Rich Can Save the World.* London: Bloomsbury.

Blagescu, M., and J. Court (2007) 'Civil society's impact on public policy', in F. Heinrich and L. Fioramonti (eds), *CIVICUS Global Survey of the State of Civil Society. Vol. 2: Comparative Perspectives.* Bloomfield, CT: Kumarian Press.

Bloch, N. (2012) 'Half-empty or half-full? Online gateways to real world action', www.WagingNonViolence.org.

Bob, C. (2005) *The Marketing of Rebellion: Insurgents, Media and International Activism.* Cambridge: Cambridge University Press.

Bob, C. (2011) 'Uncivil society', in M. Edwards (ed.), *The Oxford Handbook of Civil Society.* Oxford: Oxford University Press.

Bob, C., J. Haynes, V. Pickard, T. Keenan and N. Couldry (2007) 'Media spaces: innovation and activism', in M. Glasius, M. Kaldor and H. Anheier (eds), *Global Civil Society 2007/8.* London: Sage.

Boggs, C. (2000) *The End of Politics: Corporate Power and the Decline of the Public Sphere*. New York: Guilford Press.

Bollier, D. (2001) *Public Assets, Private Profits: Reclaiming the American Commons in an Age of Market Enclosure*. Washington, DC: New America Foundation.

Boyte, H. (2004) *Everyday Politics: Reconnecting Citizens and Public Life*. Philadelphia: University of Pennsylvania Press.

Boyte, H. (2008) *An Evaluation of Minnesota Works Together, a Movement to Transform Civic Culture in the State of Minnesota*. Minneapolis: Hubert Humphrey Institute of Public Affairs, University of Minnesota.

Boyte, H. (2011) 'Civil society and public work', in M. Edwards (ed.), *The Oxford Handbook of Civil Society*. Oxford: Oxford University Press.

Bratton, M. (1994) 'Civil society and political transition in Africa', in J. Harbeson, D. Rothschild and N. Chazan (eds), *Civil Society and the State in Africa*. Boulder, CO: Lynne Rienner.

Bugg-Levine, A., and J. Emerson (2011) *Impact Investing: Transforming How We Make Money While Making A Difference*. San Francisco: Jossey-Bass.

Building Movement Project (2006) *Social Service and Social Change: A Process Guide*. New York: Building Movement Project, www.buildingmovement.org/process_guide.pdf.

Butler, J. (2006) *Born Again: The Christian Right Globalized*. Ann Arbor: University of Michigan Press.

Campbell, D. (2002) 'Beyond charitable choice: the diverse service delivery approaches of faith-related organizations', *Non-Profit and Voluntary Sector Quarterly*, 31 (2), 207–30.

Carothers, T. (2006) *Confronting the Weakest Link: Aiding Political Parties in New Democracies*. Washington, DC: Carnegie Endowment for International Peace.

Carothers, T., and M. Ottaway (2000) *Funding Virtue: Civil Society Aid and Democracy Promotion*. Washington, DC: Carnegie Endowment for International Peace.

Carr, N. (2008) 'Is Google making us stupid?', *Atlantic Monthly* (July/August), 56–63.

Carter, S. (1999) *Civility*. New York: Harper Perennial.

Castells, M. (2012) *Networks of Outrage and Hope: Social Movements in the Internet Age*. Cambridge: Polity.

Center for Public Integrity (2002) *The Politics and Influence of the Telecommunications Industry*. Washington, DC: CPI.

Chambers, S. (2002) 'A critical theory of civil society', in S. Chambers and W. Kymlicka (eds), *Alternative Conceptions of Civil Society*. Princeton, NJ: Princeton University Press.

Chambers, S., and W. Kymlicka (eds) (2002) *Alternative Conceptions of Civil Society*. Princeton, NJ: Princeton University Press.

Chandoke, N. (2003) *The Conceits of Civil Society*. New Delhi: Oxford University Press.

Chatterjee, P. (2002) 'Civil and political society in postcolonial democracies', in S. Khilnani and S. Kaviraj (eds), *Civil Society: History and Possibilities*. Cambridge: Cambridge University Press.

Chen, M., R. Jhabvala, R. Kanbur and C. Richards (2007) *Membership-Based Organizations of the Poor*. London: Routledge.

Chetkovich, C., and F. Kunreuther (2006) *From the Ground Up: Grassroots Organizations Making Social Change*. Ithaca, NY: Cornell University Press.

Choudry, A., and D. Kapoor (2013) *NGOization: Complicity, Contradictions and Prospects*. London: Zed Books.

Christensen, H.S. (2011) 'Political activities on the Internet: slacktivism or political participation by other means?', *First Monday*, 16 (2), 2–7.

Coffe, H., and C. Bolzendahl (2011) 'Civil society and diversity', in M. Edwards (ed.), *The Oxford Handbook of Civil Society*. Oxford: Oxford University Press.

Cohen, J. (1999) 'American civil society talk', in R. Fullwinder (ed.), *Civil Society, Democracy and Civic Renewal*. Lanham, MD: Rowman & Littlefield.

Cohen, J., and A. Arato (1992) *Civil Society and Political Theory*. Cambridge, MA: MIT Press.

Comaroff, J., and J. Comaroff (eds) (1999) *Civil Society and the Political Imagination in Africa*. Chicago: University of Chicago Press.

Cornuelle, R. (1965) *Reclaiming the American Dream*. New York: Vintage.

Cross, G. (2002) *An All-Consuming Century*. New York: Columbia University Press.

Dauvergne, P., and G. LeBaron (2013) *The Corporatization of Activism*. Cambridge: Polity.

Davies, T., B. O'Connor, A. Cochran and J. Effrat (2004) *An Online Environment for Democratic Deliberation: Motivations, Principles and Design*. Stanford, CA: Stanford University, Symbolic Systems Program.

Dawson, M. (2001) *Black Visions: The Roots of Contemporary African-American Mass Political Ideologies*. Chicago: University of Chicago Press.

De Oliveira, M., and R. Tandon (eds) (1994) *Citizens Strengthening Global Civil Society*. Washington, DC: CIVICUS.

De Tocqueville, A. (1945) *Democracy in America*. 2 vols. New York: Knopf.

Dekker, P., and A. Van Den Broek (2005) 'Involvement in voluntary associations in North America and Western Europe: trends and correlates 1981–2000', *Journal of Civil Society*, 1 (1), 45–59.

Dionne, E. J. (ed.) (1998) *Community Works: The Revival of Civil Society in America*. Washington, DC: Brookings Institution Press.

Douglas, S., and S. Borgos (1996) 'Community organizing and civic renewal: a view from the south', *Social Policy* (winter), 18–28.

Dryzek, J. (2006) *Deliberative Global Politics: Discourse and Democracy in a Divided World*. Cambridge: Polity.

Dryzek, J. (2012) 'Global civil society: the progress of post-Westphalian politics', *Annual Review of Political Science*, 15, 101–19.

Eberly, D. (1998) *America's Promise: Civil Society and the Renewal of American Culture*. Lanham, MD: Rowman & Littlefield.

Eberly, D. (2008) *The Rise of Global Civil Society: Building Communities and Nations from the Bottom Up*. New York: Encounter Books.

Edwards, B., and M. Foley (2001) 'Civil society and social capital: a primer', in B. Edwards, M. Foley and M. Dani (eds), *Beyond Tocqueville: Civil Society and the Social Capital Debate in Comparative Perspective*. Hanover, NH: University Press of New England.

Edwards, B., M. Foley and M. Dani (eds) (2001) *Beyond Tocqueville: Civil Society and the Social Capital Debate in Comparative Perspective*. Hanover, NH: University Press of New England.

Edwards, M. (1999a) *Future Positive: International Cooperation in the 21st Century*. London: Earthscan.

Edwards, M. (1999b) 'NGO performance: what breeds success? New evidence from South Asia', *World Development*, 27 (2), 361–74.

Edwards, M. (2000a) 'Enthusiasts, tacticians and skeptics: civil society and social capital', *Kettering Review*, 18 (1), 39–51.

Edwards, M. (2000b) *NGO Rights and Responsibilities: A New Deal for Global Governance*. London: Foreign Policy Centre.

Edwards, M. (2001) 'Global civil society and community exchanges: a different form of movement', *Environment and Urbanization*, 13 (2), 145–9.

Edwards, M. (2007) 'Love, reason and the future of civil society', in L. McIlrath and I. MacLabhrainn (eds), *Higher Education and Civic Engagement: International Perspectives*. Aldershot: Ashgate.

Edwards, M. (2010) *Small Change: Why Business Won't Save the World*. San Francisco: Berrett-Koehler.

Edwards, M. (ed.) (2011a) *The Oxford Handbook of Civil Society*. Oxford: Oxford University Press.

Edwards, M. (2011b) 'What can the Big Society learn from history?', www.openDemocracy.net.

Edwards, M. (2013) *Beauty and the Beast: Can Money Ever Foster Social Transformation?* The Hague: Hivos.

Edwards, M., and J. Gaventa (eds) (2001) *Global Citizen Action*. Boulder, CO: Lynne Rienner; London: Earthscan.

Edwards, M., and D. Hulme (eds) (1995) *Beyond the Magic Bullet: NGO Performance and Accountability in the Post-Cold War World*. West Hartford, CT: Kumarian Press; London: Earthscan.

Edwards, M., and S. Post (eds) (2008) *The Love that Does Justice: Spiritual Activism in Dialogue with Social Science*. Cleveland: Institute for Research on Unlimited Love.

Edwards, M., and G. Sen (2000) 'NGOs, social change and the transformation of human relationships: a 21st century civic agenda', *Third World Quarterly*, 21 (4), 605–16.

Edwards, M., and S. Zadek (2003) 'Governing the provision of global public goods: the role and legitimacy of non-state actors', in I. Kaul, P. Conceiçâo, K. Le Goulven and R. Mendoza (eds), *Governing Globalization*. Oxford: Oxford University Press.

Ehrenberg, J. (1999) *Civil Society: The Critical History of an Idea*. New York: New York University Press.

Ehrenberg, J. (2011) 'The history of civil society ideas', in M. Edwards (ed.), *The Oxford Handbook of Civil Society*. Oxford: Oxford University Press.

Eidelson, J. (2013) 'Alt-labor', *American Prospect* (January/February), 15–18.

Eikenberry, A., and J. Kluwer (2004) 'The marketization of the nonprofit sector: civil society at risk?', *Public Administration Review*, 64 (2), 132–40.

El Sayed-Said, M. (2005) 'Global civil society: an Arab perspective', in M. Glasius, M. Kaldor and H. Anheier (eds), *Global Civil Society 2005/6*. London: Sage.

Eliasoph, N. (1998) *Avoiding Politics: How Americans Produce Apathy in Everyday Life*. Cambridge: Cambridge University Press.

Eliasoph, N. (2011) *Making Volunteers: Civic Life After Welfare's End*. Princeton, NJ: Princeton University Press.

Eliasoph, N. (2013) *The Politics of Volunteering*. Cambridge: Polity.

Encarnacion, O. (2011) 'Assisting civil society and promoting democracy', in M. Edwards (ed.), *The Oxford Handbook of Civil Society*. Oxford: Oxford University Press.

Escobar, A., and S. Alvarez (eds) (1992) *The Making of Social Movements in Latin America: Identity, Strategy and Democracy*. Boulder, CO: Westview Press.

Etzioni, A. (1993) *The Spirit of Community*. London: Fontana.

Evans, P. (1996) 'Development strategies across the public–private divide: introduction', *World Development*, 24 (6), 1033–7.

Ezzat, H. R. (2005) 'Beyond multicultural modernism: towards a multicultural paradigm shift in the social sciences', in M. Glasius, M. Kaldor and H. Anheier (eds), *Global Civil Society 2005/6*. London: Sage.

Falk, R. (1995) *On Humane Governance: Toward a New Global Politics*. Cambridge: Polity.

Farrell, H. (2006) 'Bloggers and parties: can the netroots reshape American democracy?', *Boston Review*, September 29.

Fiorina, M. (1999) 'Extreme voices: the dark side of civic engagement', in T. Skocpol and M. Fiorina (eds), *Civic Engagement in American Democracy*. Washington, DC: Brookings Institution Press.

Fisher, D. (2006) *Activism Inc.: How the Outsourcing of Grassroots Campaigns is Strangling Progressive Politics in America*. Stanford, CA: Stanford University Press.

Foley, M., and B. Edwards (1996) 'The paradox of civil society', *Journal of Democracy*, 7 (3), 38–52.

Foley, M., and V. Hodgkinson (eds) (2002) *The Civil Society Reader*. Hanover, NH: University Press of New England.

Forbrig, J., and P. Demes (eds) (2007) *Reclaiming Democracy: Civil Society and Electoral Change in Central and Eastern Europe*. Washington, DC: German Marshall Fund.

Fowler, A. (2004) *AID Architecture and Counter-Terrorism: Perspectives on NGO Futures*. Oxford: INTRAC.

Fowler, A. (2007) 'The challenge of socioeconomic and democratic development: marrying civil society's social and political roles?', in F. Heinrich and L. Fioramonti (eds), *CIVICUS Global Survey of the State of Civil Society. Vol. 2: Comparative Perspectives*. West Hartford, CT: Kumarian Press.

Fowler, A., and K. Biekart (eds) (2008) *Civic-Driven Change: Citizen's Imagination in Action*. The Hague: Institute of Social Studies.

Fox, J., and L. Hernandez (1992) 'Mexico's difficult democracy: grassroots movements, NGOs and local government', *Alternatives*, 17, 165–208.

Frumkin, P. (2006) *Strategic Giving: The Art and Science of Philanthropy*. Chicago: University of Chicago Press.

Fuchs, C. (2012) 'Some reflections on Manuel Castells' book *Networks of Outrage and Hope. Social Movements in the Internet Age*', *tripleC*, 10 (2), 775–97.

Fullwinder, R. (ed.) (1999) *Civil Society, Democracy and Civic Renewal*. Lanham, MD: Rowman & Littlefield.

Fung, A., and E. O. Wright (eds) (2003) *Deepening Democracy: Institutional Innovations in Empowered Participatory Governance*. London: Verso.

Galston, W. (2001) 'Political knowledge, political engagement and civic education', *Annual Review of Political Science*, 4, 217–34.

Galston, W. (2002) 'Liberal egalitarianism: a family of theories, not a single view', in R. Post and N. Rosenblum (eds), *Civil Society and Government*. Princeton, NJ: Princeton University Press.

Galston, W., and P. Levine (1998) 'America's civic condition: a glance at the evidence', in E. J. Dionne (ed.), *Community Works*. Washington, DC: Brookings Institution Press.

Gellner, E. (1994) *Conditions of Liberty: Civil Society and its Rivals*. London: Hamish Hamilton.

Georgetown University Center for Social Impact Communication (2011) *Dynamics of Cause Engagement*. Washington, DC: Georgetown University.

Geremek, B. (1992) *The Idea of Civil Society*. Research Triangle Park, NC: National Humanities Center.

Giddens, A. (ed.) (2001) *The Global Third Way Debate*. Cambridge: Polity.

Giugni, M. (1999) 'How social movements matter', in M. Giugni, D. McAdam and C. Tilly (eds), *How Social Movements Matter*. Minneapolis: University of Minnesota Press.

Glasius, M. (2008) 'Does the involvement of global civil society make international decision-making more democratic? The case of the International Criminal Court', *Journal of Civil Society*, 4 (1), 43–60.

Glasius, M., and J. Timms (2005) 'Social forums: radical beacon or strategic infrastructure?', in M. Glasius, M. Kaldor and H. Anheier (eds), *Global Civil Society 2005/6*. London: Sage.

Glasius, M., M. Kaldor and H. Anheier (eds) (2003) *Global Civil Society 2002/3*. Oxford: Oxford University Press.

Glasius, M., M. Kaldor and H. Anheier (eds) (2004) *Global Civil Society 2004/5*. Oxford: Oxford University Press.

Glasius, M., M. Kaldor and H. Anheier (eds) (2005) *Global Civil Society 2005/6*. London: Sage.

Glasius, M., M. Kaldor and H. Anheier (eds) (2006) *Global Civil Society 2006/7*. London: Sage.

Glasius, M., M. Kaldor and H. Anheier (eds) (2007) *Global Civil Society 2007/8*. London: Sage.

Global Partners and Associates (2007) *New Threats and Opportunities for Freedom of Expression in the Global Information Society*. London: Global Partners.

Goody, J. (2002) 'Civil society in an extra-European perspective', in S. Khilnani and S. Kaviraj (eds), *Civil Society: History and Possibilities*. Cambridge: Cambridge University Press.

Gottesdiener, L. (2012) 'A new face of the new labor movement', www.WagingNonViolence.org.

Grootaert, C. (1999) *Does Social Capital Help the Poor? A Synthesis of Findings from the Local-Level Institutions Study in Bolivia, Burkina Faso and Indonesia*. Washington, DC: World Bank.

Guardian (2013). 'IRS chief says tax-exemption screening went wider than Tea Party groups', *Guardian*, June 24, http://www.guardian.co.uk/world/2013/jun/24/irs-chief-tea-party-occupy-tax.

Guinness, O. (2008) *The Case for Civility and Why Our Future Depends on It*. New York: HarperOne.

Hagemann, K., S. Michel and G. Budde (eds) (2008) *Civil Society and Gender Justice*. London: Berghahn Books.

Hall, H., and S. Perry (2013) 'Girl Scouts financial and leadership woes threaten 100-year-old group', *Chronicle of Philanthropy*, April 7.

Hall, J. (ed.) (1995) *Civil Society: Theory, History, Comparison*. Cambridge: Polity.

Hall, J., and F. Trentmann (eds) (2005) *Civil Society: A Reader in History, Theory and Global Politics*. Basingstoke: Palgrave Macmillan.

Hampshire, S. (1999) *Justice is Conflict*. Princeton, NJ: Princeton University Press.

Hann, C. (2004) 'In the church of civil society', in M. Glasius, M. Kaldor and H. Anheier (eds), *Global Civil Society 2004/5*. Oxford: Oxford University Press.

Hann, C., and E. Dunn (eds) (1996) *Civil Society: Challenging Western Models*. London: Routledge.

Harbeson, J., D. Rothschild and N. Chazan (eds) (1994) *Civil Society and the State in Africa*. Boulder, CO: Lynne Rienner.

Harris, F. (1999) 'Will the circle be unbroken? The erosion and transformation of African-American civic life', in R. Fullwinder (ed.), *Civil Society, Democracy and Civic Renewal*. Lanham, MD: Rowman & Littlefield.

Harris, J. (2001) *Depoliticizing Development: The World Bank and Social Capital*. New Delhi: Lectword Books.

Hashemi, S. (1997) 'Building NGO legitimacy in Bangladesh', in D. Lewis (ed.), *International Perspectives on Voluntary Action*. London: Earthscan.

Hassabo, C. (2007) *The Vicissitudes of Grassroots Democracy: The Case of the Bloggers, Kefaya and the Mahalla Textile Company Workers*. Cairo: Ford Foundation.

Hassan, K. (2012) 'Making sense of the Arab Spring: listening to the voices of Middle Eastern activists', *Development*, 55 (2), 232–8.

Hawken, P. (2007) *Blessed Unrest: How the Largest Movement in the World Came into Being and Why No One Saw it Coming*. New York: Penguin.

Hawthorne, A. (2004) *Middle Eastern Democracy: Is Civil Society the Answer?* Democracy and Rule of Law Project, Paper No. 44. Washington, DC: Carnegie Endowment for International Peace.

Hearn, J. (2001) 'The uses and abuses of civil society in Africa', *Review of African Political Economy*, 28 (87), 43–53.

Heinrich, V. F. (2008) 'Studying civil society across the world: exploring the thorny issues of conceptualization and measurement', *Journal of Civil Society*, 1 (3), 211–28.

Heinrich, V. F., and L. Fioramonti (eds) (2007) *CIVICUS Global Survey of the State of Civil Society. Vol. 2: Comparative Perspectives*. Bloomfield, CT: Kumarian Press.

Heller, P. (1996) 'Social capital as a product of class mobilization and state intervention: industrial workers in Kerala, India', *World Development*, 24 (6), 1055–71.

Henderson, S. (2003) *Building Democracy in Contemporary Russia: Western Support for Grassroots Organizations*. Ithaca, NY: Cornell University Press.

Henriksen, L. S., and L. Svedberg (2010) 'Volunteering and social activism: moving beyond the traditional divide', *Journal of Civil Society*, 6 (2), 95–8.

Hill, G. (2008) 'A case of NGO participation: the ICC negotiations', in J. Walker and A. Thompson (eds), *Critical Mass: The Emergence of Global Civil Society*. Toronto: Wilfred Laurier University Press.

Hirschman, A. (1970) *Exit, Voice and Loyalty: Responses to Decline in Firms, Organizations and States*. Cambridge, MA: Harvard University Press.

Hirst, P. (1994) *Associative Democracy: New Forms of Economic and Social Governance*. Cambridge: Polity.

Howell, J. (2005) 'Gender and civil society', in M. Glasius, M. Kaldor and H. Anheier (eds), *Global Civil Society 2005/6*. London: Sage.

Howell, J., and J. Pearce (2001) *Civil Society and Development: A Critical Exploration*. Boulder, CO: Lynne Rienner.

Hulme, D., and M. Edwards (eds) (1997) *NGOs, States and Donors: Too Close for Comfort?* New York and London: Palgrave Macmillan.

Ibrahim, S. (1995) 'Civil society and the prospects for democracy in the Arab world', in A. Norton (ed.), *Civil Society in the Middle East*. Leiden: E. J. Brill.

INCITE (2007) *The Revolution Will Not Be Funded: Beyond the Non-Profit Industrial Complex*. Cambridge, MA: South End Press.

International Center for Not-for-Profit Law (2013) *NGO Law Monitor*. Washington, DC: ICNL.

Isaac, J. (1998) *Democracy in Dark Times*. Ithaca, NY: Cornell University Press.

Jalali, R. (2005) 'Foreign aid and civil society: how external aid is detrimental to southern NGOs and social movements', *Democracy and Society*, 2 (2), 6–24.

Jenkins, R. (2002) 'Mistaking "governance" for "politics": foreign aid, democracy and the contribution of civil society', in

S. Khilnani and S. Kaviraj (eds), *Civil Society: History and Possibilities*. Cambridge: Cambridge University Press.

Johnson, B. (2002) *Objective Hope: Assessing the Effectiveness of Faith-Based Organizations: A Review of the Literature*. Philadelphia: University of Pennsylvania, Center for Research on Religion and Urban Civil Society.

Johnson, S. (2013) *Future Perfect: The Case for Progress in a Networked Age*. New York: Riverhead.

Jordan, J. (1992) *Technical Difficulties: African-American Notes on the State of the Union*. New York: Pantheon.

Jordan, L. (2011) 'Global civil society', in M. Edwards (ed.), *The Oxford Handbook of Civil Society*. Oxford: Oxford University Press.

Jordan, L., and P. van Tuijl (eds) (2006) *NGO Accountability: Politics, Principles and Innovations*. London: Earthscan.

Kahne, J., N. Lee and J. Feezell (2013) 'The civic and political significance of online participatory cultures among youth transitioning to adulthood', *Journal of Information Technology and Politics*, 10 (1), 1–20.

Kaldor, M. (2003) *Global Civil Society*. Cambridge: Polity.

Kandil, A. (1995) *Civil Society in the Arab World*. Washington, DC: Civicus.

Keane, J. (1998) *Civil Society: Old Images, New Visions*. Stanford, CA: Stanford University Press.

Keane, J. (2003) *Global Civil Society*. Cambridge: Cambridge University Press.

Kelsay, J. (2002) 'Civil society and government in Islam', in R. Post and N. Rosenblum (eds), *Civil Society and Government*. Princeton, NJ: Princeton University Press.

Khagram, S., and S. Alvord (2006) 'The rise of civic transnationalism', in S. Batliwala and L. D. Brown (eds), *Transnational Civil Society: An Introduction*. Bloomfield, CT: Kumarian Press.

Khalaf, S. (2002) *Civil and Uncivil Violence in Lebanon: A History of the Internationalization of Communal Conflict in Lebanon*. New York: Columbia University Press.

Khallaf, M., and O. Tur (2007) 'Civil society in the Middle East and Mediterranean', in V. F. Heinrich and L. Fioramonti (eds), *CIVICUS Global Survey of the State of Civil Society. Vol. 2: Comparative Perspectives*. Bloomfield, CT: Kumarian Press.

Khilnani, S. (2002) 'The development of civil society', in S. Khilnani and S. Kaviraj (eds), *Civil Society: History and Possibilities*. Cambridge: Cambridge University Press.

Khilnani, S., and S. Kaviraj (eds) (2002) *Civil Society: History and Possibilities*. Cambridge: Cambridge University Press.

Kienle, E. (2012) 'Egypt without Mubarak, Tunisia after Bin Ali: theory, history and the Arab Spring', *Economy and Society*, 41 (4), 532–57.

Konrád, G. (1989) *Antipolitics*. New York: Bookthrift.

Kopecky, P., and C. Mudde (2007) 'Civil or uncivil? Civil society's role in promoting values, norms and rights', in F. V. Heinrich and L. Fioramonti (eds), *CIVICUS Global Survey of the State of Civil Society. Vol. 2: Comparative Perspectives*. Bloomfield, CT: Kumarian Press.

Ladd, E. (1999) *The Ladd Report*. New York: Free Press.

Lanier, J. (2011) *You Are Not a Gadget: A Manifesto*. New York: Vintage.

Lanier, J. (2013) *Who Owns the Future?* New York: Simon & Schuster.

Larson, S. (2006) 'The World Social Forum in search of itself', *openDemocracy*, January 26, www.opendemocracy.net/globalization-world/wsf_3211.jsp.

Lasch, C. (1996) *The Revolt of the Elites and the Betrayal of Democracy*. New York: W. W. Norton.

Leadbeater, C. (2008) *We-Think*. London: Profile.

Lehman, H. (2008) 'The emergence of civil society organizations in South Africa', *Journal of Public Affairs*, 8, 115–27.

Leighninger, M. (2006) *The Next Form of Democracy: How Expert Rule is Giving Way to Shared Governance and Why Politics Will Never Be the Same*. Nashville: Vanderbilt University Press.

Lentz, R. (2011) 'Civil society in the digital age', in M. Edwards (ed.), *The Oxford Handbook of Civil Society*. Oxford: Oxford University Press.

Lessig, L. (2001) *The Future of Ideas: The Fate of the Commons in a Connected World*. New York: Random House.

Levi, M. (1996) 'Social and unsocial capital: review of *Making Democracy Work*', *Politics and Society*, 24 (1), 45–55.

Levine, P. (2002) *Building the Electronic Commons*. College Park: University of Maryland, Democracy Collaborative, http://democracycollaborative.umd.edu/programs/public/Building ElectronicCommons.pdf.

Levine, P. (2007) *The Future of Democracy: Developing the Next Generation of American Citizens.* Hanover, NH: University Press of New England.

Lewis, D. (2002) 'Civil society in African contexts: reflections on the usefulness of a concept', *Development and Change*, 33 (4), 569–86.

Lewis, D. (2004) 'Old and new civil societies in Bangladesh', in M. Glasius, D. Lewis and H. Seckinelgin (eds), *Exploring Civil Society: Political and Cultural Contexts*. Abingdon: Routledge.

Lewis, D. (2008) 'Crossing the boundaries between third sector and state: life-work histories from the Philippines, Bangladesh and the UK', *Third World Quarterly*, 29 (1), 125–41.

Li, X. (1999) 'Democracy and uncivil societies: a critique of civil society determinism', in R. Fullwinder (ed.), *Civil Society, Democracy and Civic Renewal*. Lanham, MD: Rowman & Littlefield.

Lichtenstein, N. (2002) *State of the Union: A Century of American Labor*. Princeton, NJ: Princeton University Press.

Lichterman, P. (2005) *Elusive Togetherness: Church Groups Trying to Bridge America's Divisions*. Princeton, NJ: Princeton University Press.

Lievrouw, L. (2011) *Alternative and Activist New Media*. Cambridge: Polity.

Lohmann, R., and J. Van Til (eds) (2012) *Resolving Community Conflicts and Problems: Public Deliberation and Sustained Dialogue*. New York: Columbia University Press.

Long, S. (2000) *The New Student Politics: The Wingspread Statement on Student Civic Engagement*. Washington, DC: Campus Compact.

Lutsevych, O. (2013) *How to Finish a Revolution: Civil Society and Democracy in Georgia, Moldova and Ukraine*. Chatham House Briefing Paper 2013/01. London: Chatham House.

Majed, Z. (1998) 'Civil society in Lebanon', *Kettering Review* (fall), 36–43.

Mamdani, M. (1996) *Citizen and Subject: Contemporary Africa and the Legacy of Late Colonialism*. Princeton, NJ: Princeton University Press.

Mardin, S. (1995) 'Civil society and Islam', in J. Hall (ed.), *Civil Society: Theory, History, Comparison*. Cambridge: Polity.

Marquand, D. (2004) *Decline of the Public: The Hollowing Out of Citizenship*. Cambridge: Polity.

Mathews, J. (1997) 'Power shift', *Foreign Affairs* (January/February), 50–66.

Mau, S., J. Mewes and A. Zimmerman (2008) 'Cosmopolitan attitudes through transnational social practices?', *Global Networks*, 8 (1), 1–24.

McBride, A. M., and M. Sherraden (eds) (2007) *Civic Service Worldwide: Impacts and Inquiry*. London: M. E. Sharpe.

McChesney, R. (2013) *Digital Disconnect: How Capitalism is Turning the Internet Against Democracy*. New York: the New Press.

McClain, L., and J. Fleming (2000) 'Some questions for civil society revivalists', *Chicago-Kent Law Review*, 75 (2), 301–54.

McConnell, C. (2003) 'Advanced democracy', *YES Magazine* (winter), 41–2.

McFarland, D., and R. Thomas (2006) 'Bowling young: how youth voluntary associations influence adult political participation', *American Sociological Review*, 71 (June), 401–25.

McPherson, M., L. Smith-Lovin and M. Brashears (2006) 'Social isolation in America: changes in core discussion networks over two decades', *American Sociological Review*, 71 (June), 353–75.

Mertes, T. (2002) 'Grassroots globalism: reply to Michael Hardt', *New Left Review*, 17 (September/October), 101–10.

Metzger, T. (2002) 'The Western concept of civil society in the context of Chinese history', in S. Khilnani and S. Kaviraj (eds), *Civil Society: History and Possibilities*. Cambridge: Cambridge University Press.

Meyer, M., and C. Hyde (2004) 'Too much of a good thing? Insular neighbourhood associations, nonreciprocal civility and the promotion of civic health', *Non-Profit and Voluntary Sector Quarterly*, 33 (3), 77–96.

Minkoff, D. (2002a) 'The emergence of hybrid organizational forms: combining identity-based service provision and political action', *Non-Profit and Voluntary Sector Quarterly*, 31 (5), 377–401.

Minkoff, D. (2002b) 'Walking a political tightrope: responsiveness and internal accountability in social movement organizations', in E. Reid and M. Montilla (eds), *Exploring Organizations and Advocacy: Governance and Accountability*. Washington, DC: Urban Institute.

Morozov, E. (2011) *The Net Delusion: The Dark Side of Internet Freedom*. New York: Public Affairs.

Morozov, E. (2013) *To Save Everything, Click Here: The Folly of Technological Solutionism*. New York: Public Affairs.

Morton, D. (2006) 'Gunning for the world', *Foreign Policy* (January/ February), 58–67.

Muasher, M. (2011) 'Arab Spring: eternal season of flux', *Politico*, June 30.

Mutz, D. (2006) *Hearing the Other Side: Deliberative versus Participatory Democracy*. Cambridge: Cambridge University Press.

Myers, S. (1996) *Democracy is a Discussion: Civic Engagement in Old and New Democracies*. New London: Connecticut College.

National Council of Voluntary Organizations (2012) *What the Research Tells Us About the Voluntary Sector*, http://www .ncvo-vol.org.uk/policy-research/what-voluntary-sector/what -research-tells-us.

Nicholls, A. (2011) 'Social enterprise and social entrepreneurs', in M. Edwards (ed.), *The Oxford Handbook of Civil Society*. Oxford: Oxford University Press.

Nosco, P. (2002) 'Confucian perspectives on civil society and government', in R. Post and N. Rosenblum (eds), *Civil Society and Government*. Princeton, NJ: Princeton University Press.

Obadare, E. (2011) 'Civil society in Africa', in M. Edwards (ed.), *The Oxford Handbook of Civil Society*. Oxford: Oxford University Press.

O'Connell, B. (1999) *Civil Society: The Underpinnings of American Democracy*. Hanover, NH: University Press of New England.

Orvis, S. (2001) 'Civil society in Africa or African civil society?', *Journal of Asian and African Studies*, 36 (1), 17–38.

Patel, S., J. Bolnick and D. Mitlin (2001) 'Squatting on the global highway: community exchanges for urban transformation', in M. Edwards and J. Gaventa (eds), *Global Citizen Action*. Boulder, CO: Lynne Rienner; London: Earthscan.

Paya, A. (2004) 'Civil society in Iran: past, present and future', in M. Glasius, D. Lewis and H Seckinelgin (eds), *Exploring Civil Society: Political and Cultural Contexts*. Abingdon: Routledge.

Peklo, J. (2004) *The Balkan Syndrome: Nationalism and the Media*. Krakow: ZNAK Foundation.

Perez-Diaz, V. (1993) *The Return of Civil Society: The Emergence of Democratic Spain*. Cambridge, MA: Harvard University Press.

Peters, P., and J. Scarpacci (1998) *Cuba's New Entrepreneurs: Five Years of Small-Scale Capitalism*. Arlington, VA: Alexis de Tocqueville Institution.

Pew Research Center's Internet and American Life Project (2011) *The Social Impact of Technology*. Washington, DC: Pew Research Center.

Pianta, M. (2005) *UN World Summits and Civil Society: The State of the Art*. Civil Society and Social Movements Paper no. 18. Geneva: United Nations Research Institute on Social Development.

Post, R., and N. Rosenblum (eds) (2002) *Civil Society and Government*. Princeton, NJ: Princeton University Press.

Price, V. (2007) 'Democracy, global publics and world opinion', in M. Glasius, M. Kaldor and H. Anheier (eds), *Global Civil Society 2007/8*. London: Sage.

Pritchett, L., and D. Kaufman (1998) 'Civil liberties, democracy and the performance of government projects', *Finance and Development* (March), 26–9.

Pushback Network (2008) *All Together Now*. Los Angeles: Pushback Network.

Putnam, R. (1993) *Making Democracy Work: Civic Traditions in Modern Italy*. Princeton, NJ: Princeton University Press.

Putnam, R. (2000) *Bowling Alone: The Collapse and Revival of American Community*. New York: Simon & Schuster.

Putnam, R. (2007) 'E pluribus unum: diversity and community in the twenty-first century', *Scandinavian Political Studies*, 30 (2), 137–74.

Ramesh, R. (2007) 'Nobel winner starts anti-graft party', *Guardian Weekly*, March 2–8.

Ray, M. (2002) *The Changing and Unchanging Face of US Civil Society*. New Brunswick, NJ: Transaction.

Read, B., and R. Pekkanen (2008) *Straddling State and Society: Challenges and Insights from Ambiguous Associations*. Iowa City: Department of Political Science, University of Iowa.

Reilly, C. (ed.) (1995) *New Paths to Democratic Development in Latin America: The Rise of NGO–Municipal Collaboration*. Boulder, CO: Lynne Rienner.

Rieff, D. (1999) 'The false dawn of civil society', *Nation*, February 22.

Rifkin, J. (1995) *The End of Work: The Decline of the Global Labor Force and the Dawn of the Post-Market Era*. New York: G. P. Putnam.

Robin, C. (2001) 'Missing the point: a review of *Bowling Alone*', *Dissent* (spring), 108–11.

Rodriguez, L. (2007) 'The Girl Scouts: uncharted territory', *Non-Profit Quarterly* (fall), 16–22.

Roepke, W. (1996) *The Moral Foundations of Civil Society*. New Brunswick, NJ: Transaction.

Rosen, J. (2001) *What Are Journalists For?* New Haven, CT: Yale University Press.

Rosenblum, N. (1998) *Membership and Morals: The Personal Uses of Pluralism in America*. Princeton, NJ: Princeton University Press.

Rosenblum, N. (1999) 'The moral uses of pluralism', in R. Fullwinder (ed.), *Civil Society, Democracy and Civic Renewal*. Lanham, MD: Rowman & Littlefield.

Rutenberg, J. (2002) 'A foundation travels far from Sesame Street', *New York Times*, September 6.

Salam, N. (2002) *Civil Society in the Arab World: The Historical and Political Dimensions*. Occasional Paper 3, Islamic Legal Studies Program, Harvard Law School.

Salamon, L. (1993) *The Global Associational Revolution: The Rise of the Third Sector on the World Scene*. Occasional Paper 15. Baltimore: Johns Hopkins University, Institute for Policy Studies.

Salamon, L. (2004) *Global Civil Society: Dimensions of the Nonprofit Sector. Vol. 2*. West Hartford, CT: Kumarian Press.

Salamon, L. (2010) 'Putting the civil society sector on the economic map of the world,' *Annals of Public and Cooperative Economics*, 81 (2), 167–211.

Salem, P. (1998) 'Deconstructing civil society: reflections on a paradigm', *Kettering Review* (fall), 8–15.

Sampson, S. (1996) 'The social life of projects: importing civil society to Albania', in C. Hann and E. Dunn (eds), *Civil Society: Challenging Western Models*. London: Routledge.

Schattan, V., P. Coelho and B. von Lieres (2010) *Mobilizing for Democracy: Citizen Action and the Politics of Public Participation*. London: Zed Books.

Schlumberger, O. (ed.) (2007) *Debating Arab Authoritarianism: Dynamics and Durability in Non-Democratic Regimes*. Stanford, CA: Stanford University Press.

Schmidt, E., and J. Cohen (2013) *The New Digital Age: Reshaping the Future of People, Nations and Business*. New York: Knopf.

Scholte, J. (2002) *Democratizing the Global Economy: The Role of Civil Society*. Coventry: University of Warwick, Centre for the Study of Globalization.

Scholte, J. (2007) 'Civil society and the legitimization of global governance', *Journal of Civil Society*, 3 (3), 305–26.

Scholte, J. (2008) 'Looking to the future: a global civil society forum', in J. Walker and A. Thompson (eds), *Critical Mass: The Emergence of Global Civil Society*. Toronto: Wilfred Laurier University Press.

Seckinelgin, H. (2004) 'Contractions of a sociocultural reflex: civil society in Turkey', in M. Glasius, D. Lewis and H. Seckinelgin (eds), *Exploring Civil Society: Political and Cultural Contexts*. Abingdon: Routledge.

Sehm-Patomaki, K., and M. Ulvila (2006) *Democratic Politics Globally: Elements for a Dialogue on Global Political Party Formations*. Working Paper 1. Helsinki: Network Institute for Global Democratization.

Seligman, A. (1992) *The Idea of Civil Society*. Princeton, NJ: Princeton University Press.

Seligman, A. (2002) 'Civil society as idea and ideal', in S. Chambers and W. Kymlicka (eds), *Alternative Conceptions of Civil Society*. Princeton, NJ: Princeton University Press.

Senzai, F. (2004) 'Bush's shaky plans for change in the Middle East', *Civility Review*, 1 (1), 3–4.

Shaaban, A. B. (2007) 'The new protest movements in Egypt: has the country lost patience?', *Arab Reform Brief*, 17 (November).

Shah, N., and F. Jansen (2011) *Digital Alternatives With a Cause*. The Hague: Hivos.

Shirky, C. (2008) *Here Comes Everybody: The Power of Organizing without Organizations*. London: Allen Lane.

Shirky, C. (2010) *Cognitive Surplus: Creativity and Generosity in a Connected Age*. New York: Penguin.

Sidel, M. (2004) *More Secure, Less Free? Antiterrorism Policy and Civil Liberties after September 11*. Ann Arbor: University of Michigan Press.

Singer, P. (2002) *One World: The Ethics of Globalization*. New Haven, CT: Yale University Press.

Skocpol, T. (1999) 'Advocates without members: the recent transformation of American civic life', in T. Skocpol and M. Fiorina (eds), *Civic Engagement in American Democracy*. Washington, DC: Brookings Institution Press.

Skocpol, T. (2003) *Diminished Democracy: From Membership to Management in American Civic Life*. Oklahoma City: University of Oklahoma Press.

Skocpol, T., and M. Fiorina (1999) 'Making sense of the civic engagement debate', in T. Skocpol and M. Fiorina (eds), *Civic Engagement in American Democracy*. Washington, DC: Brookings Institution Press.

Skocpol, T., and W. Williamson (2012) *The Tea Party and the Remaking of Republican Conservatism*. Oxford: Oxford University Press.

Slaughter, A.-M. (2004) *A New World Order*. Princeton, NJ: Princeton University Press.

Smillie, I. (1996) *Service Delivery or Civil Society? NGOs in Bosnia and Hercegovina*. Ottawa: CARE Canada.

Smith, D. H. (2000) *Grassroots Associations*. Thousand Oaks, CA: Sage.

Smith, R. (1996) *We Have No Leaders: African Americans in the Post-Civil Rights Era*. Albany: SUNY Press.

Sogge, D. (2006) 'African civil domains: realities and mirages', in *Crisis of the State and Civil Domains in Africa*. Madrid: FRIDE.

Strauss, A., and R. Falk (1997) 'For a global peoples' assembly', *International Herald Tribune*, November 14.

Surman, M., and K. Reilly (2003) *Appropriating the Internet for Social Change*. New York: Social Science Research Council.

Tamman, H. (2008) 'Repentant Jihadists and the changing face of Islam', *Arab Reform Bulletin* (September), http://carnegieendowment.org/2008/09/09/repentant-jihadists-and-changing-face-of-islamism-in-egypt/eiaa.

Tarrow, S. (1996) 'Making social science work across space and time: a critical reflection on Robert Putnam's *Making Democracy Work*', *American Political Science Review*, 90 (2), 389–97.

Tarrow, S. (1998) *Power in Movement: Social Movements and Contentious Politics*. Cambridge: Cambridge University Press.

Tarrow, S. (2005) *The New Transnational Activism*. Cambridge: Cambridge University Press.

Tarrow, S. (2012) *Strangers at the Gates: Movements and States in Contentious Politics*. Cambridge: Cambridge University Press.

Tendler, J. (1996) *Good Government in the Tropics*. Cambridge, MA: MIT Press.

Thompson, A. (2008) 'A global civil society forum: laying the groundwork', in J. Walker and A. Thompson (eds), *Critical Mass: The Emergence of Global Civil Society*. Toronto: Wilfred Laurier University Press.

Tilly, C. (2007) *Democracy*. Cambridge: Cambridge University Press.

Tilly, C., and S. Tarrow (2007) *Contentious Politics*. London: Paradigm.

Turkle, S. (2011) *Alone Together: Why We Expect More from Technology and Less from Each Other*. New York: Basic Books.

Unger, J. (ed.) (2008) *Associations and the Chinese State: Contested Spaces*. London: M. E. Sharpe.

United States Department of State (2012) *Fact Sheet on NGOs in the United States*, http://www.humanrights.gov/2012/01/12/fact-sheet-non-governmental-organizations-ngos-in-the-united-states.

UNRISD (2005) *World Summits and Civil Society Engagement*. Research and Policy Brief 6. Geneva: United Nations Research Institute for Social Development.

Uphoff, N. (1993) 'Grassroots organizations and NGOs in rural development: opportunities with diminishing states and expanding markets', *World Development*, 21 (4), 607–22.

Uvin, P. (1998) *Aiding Violence: The Development Enterprise in Rwanda*. West Hartford, CT: Kumarian Press.

Van der Veer, P. (2002) 'Civic calm', *Biblio* (November/December), 34–5.

Van Gelder, S. (2011) *This Changes Everything*. San Francisco: Berrett Koehler.

Van Rooy, A. (ed.) (1998) *Civil Society and the Aid Industry*. London: Earthscan.

Van Rooy, A. (2004) *The Global Legitimacy Game: Civil Society, Globalization and Protest*. Basingstoke: Palgrave Macmillan.

Varshney, A. (2002) *Ethnic Conflict and Civic Life: Hindus and Muslims in India*. New Haven, CT: Yale University Press.

Verba, S., K. Schlozman and H. Brady (1995) *Voice and Equality: Civic Voluntarism in American Politics*. Cambridge, MA: Harvard University Press.

Verba, S., K. Schlozman and H. Brady (2012) *The Un-Heavenly Chorus: Unequal Political Voice and the Broken Promise of American Democracy*. Princeton, NJ: Princeton University Press.

Walker, J., and A. Thompson (eds) (2008) *Critical Mass: The Emergence of Global Civil Society*. Toronto: Wilfred Laurier University Press.

Walzer, M. (1998) 'The idea of civil society: a path to social reconstruction', in E. J. Dionne (ed.), *Community Works: The Revival of Civil Society in America*. Washington, DC: Brookings Institution Press.

Wang, T., and R. Winn (2006) *Groundswell Meets Groundwork: Recommendations for Building on Immigrant Mobilizations*. New York: Four Freedoms Fund.

Warren, M. (2001a) *Democracy and Association*. Princeton, NJ: Princeton University Press.

Warren, M. (2001b) *Dry Bones Rattling: Community Building to Revitalize American Democracy*. Princeton, NJ: Princeton University Press.

Wasserman, D. (1999) 'Self-help groups, community and civil society', in R. Fullwinder (ed.), *Civil Society, Democracy and Civic Renewal*. Lanham, MD: Rowman & Littlefield.

Weisbrod, B. (2004) 'The pitfalls of profits: why nonprofits should get out of commercial ventures', *Stanford Social Innovation Review*, 2 (3), 1–8.

Whitaker, C., B. de Sousa Santos and B. Cassen (2005) 'The World Social Forum: where do we stand and where are we going?', in M. Glasius, M. Kaldor and H. Anheier (eds), *Global Civil Society 2005/6*. London: Sage.

White, G. (1994) 'Civil society, democratization and development: clearing the analytical ground', *Democratization*, 1 (3), 375–90.

White, J. (1996) 'Civic culture and Islam in urban Turkey', in C. Hann and E. Dunn (eds), *Civil Society: Challenging Western Models*. London: Routledge.

Widener Law Review (2007) *Symposium on Envisioning a More Democratic Global System*, *Widener Law Review*, 13 (2), 1–446.

Wilson, J. (2006) 'Civil society: a Russian variant?', *openDemocracy*, June 17, www.opendemocracy.net/Russia/article/Civil-Society -A-Russian-Variant.

Wing, K., T. Pollak and A. Blackwood (2008) *The NonProfit Almanac 2008*. Washington, DC: Urban Institute Press.

Wolfe, A. (1998) 'Is civil society obsolete?', in E. J. Dionne (ed.), *Community Works: The Revival of Civil Society in America*. Washington, DC: Brookings Institution Press.

Woolcock, M. (1998) 'Social capital and economic development: toward a theoretical synthesis and policy framework', *Theory and Society*, 27 (2), 151–208.

Wuthnow, R. (2007) *America and the Challenges of Religious Diversity*. Princeton, NJ: Princeton University Press.

Xiaoguang, K. (2002) *An Evaluation of the State of Development of Chinese NGOs and Suggestions for Capacity-Building.* Beijing: Chinese Academy of Sciences Research Centre.

Zadek, S. (2001) *The Civil Corporation.* London: Earthscan.

Zubaida, S. (2002) 'Civil society, community and democracy in the Middle East', in S. Khilnani and S. Kaviraj (eds), *Civil Society: History and Possibilities.* Cambridge: Cambridge University Press.

Index